The Principal as
Chief Executive Officer

Dedicated To

My wife Jane, and daughters Lauren, Erica and Katie for their constant guidance, support and dedication.

The Principal as Chief Executive Officer

Edited by
Andrew E. Dubin, PhD
San Francisco State University

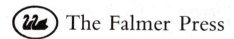 The Falmer Press

(A member of the Taylor & Francis Group)
London · New York · Philadelphia

UK   The Falmer Press, 4 John St, London WC1N 2ET
USA   The Falmer Press, Taylor & Francis Inc., 1900 Frost Road,
      Suite 101, Bristol, PA 19007

First published 1991

British Library Cataloguing in Publication Data
The principal as chief education officer.
  1. United States. Schools. Management. Leadership
  I. Dubin, Andrew E.
  371.200973

  ISBN 1-85000-805-1
  ISBN 1-85000-860-X pbk

Library of Congress Cataloging-in-Publication Data
The Principal as chief executive officer/Andrew E. Dubin,
    editor.
    p.   cm.
  Includes index.
  ISBN 1-85000-805-1: — ISBN 1-85000-806-X (pbk.):
    1. School principals—United States.   2. School management
  and organization—United States.   I. Dubin, Andrew E.
  LB2831.92.P73   1991
  371.2'012'0973—dc20   90-48611
                                                         CIP

Jacket design by Caroline Archer

Typeset in 10.5/12 pt Bembo by
Graphicraft Typesetters Ltd., Hong Kong

*Printed in Great Britain by Burgess Science Press, Basingstoke
on paper which has a specified pH value on final paper
manufacture of not less than 7.5 and is therefore 'acid free'.*

Contents

Contents

In Memory of George Hallowitz

This anthology would not have been possible without the support, assistance and vision of Professor George Hallowitz who assisted me in co-writing the Introduction. His analytic skill and keen sense of people and decision making made this undertaking both substantive and unique. He will always be missed.

Preface

This book was predicated on the idea that an effective principal must be proactive in decision making and have available appropriate information sources to make that process viable. In order to test the efficacy of that idea, analyses of decision making were conducted on a multitude of levels and by a number of professionals in the field.

The richness of the content of the book was augmented by the personal accounts offered by the contributing authors as they described their decision-making situations or discussed their perceptions regarding our educational system. In each case, while they focused on the types of approaches and strategies that were employed in order to arrive at an appropriate decision as well as information sources that were needed to make those decisions, there was a layer of the personal, more subjective feeling that underscored those decisions. No doubt, these personal perspectives of the situations were factored into these decisions and added a more complete picture.

This is a book that offers a range of decision-making situations by those whose careers are defined by how well they identify and execute those decisions. Each author speaks to this within the context of his or her own situation (which always has generic implications) but discusses it in a reflective way. While a main thrust of the book deals with the decision-making processes on the part of the principals of K–12 school settings and how information was utilized in those efforts, not all those who wrote the chapters or were interviewed were principals, for example, chief executive officers (CEOs), educational administrative professors and teachers. For this reason the book's content has considerable range and scope. Interestingly, there are very distinct and unifying characteristics about decision making which emerge from all the information sources utilized in order to make those decisions.

This book is appropriate for the education and training of those aspiring to become decision makers in our educational system, that is, principals, assistant principals, vice principals, district-level project directors, coordinators, etc. I believe it will also be exceedingly useful for those already employed in such positions because it offers an excursion into the processes and outcomes of decision making by those who have been identified as excellent leaders, that is, decision makers, in K-12 schools, districts, universities and private enterprises. Having the thoughts and experiences of CEOs from both the private and public institutions, exemplary principals, university professors, and teachers impacted by these decisions, within one anthology, is uniquely informative.

In addition to those contributing authors identified in the text, the editor wishes to thank those people who also helped to make this project possible: Professors Jack Fraenkel and Norm Wallen, whose support and expertise were always available and greatly appreciated; John Biddle, whose guidance, expertise and wisdom were invaluable throughout the development of the manuscript; and John Loomis, whose technical assistance, editing and general feedback were extremely helpful in reviewing and formulating the document.

Andrew E. Dubin

Chapter 1

General Introduction

Overview

What makes an effective principal? In the continuous wave of educational reform reports — The Carnegie Forum on Education and the Economy, The Holmes Group, The Commons Commission Report, and The Report of the National Commission on Excellence in Educational Administration — successful schools are realized, in large part, because of the efforts of the principal at the school. Terms such as instructional manager, inspirational leader, manager of resources, organizational expert, cultural leader, teacher advocate have been used when describing, or at least, labeling an effective principal. We know, based upon volumes of research-based information, that effective principals create an atmosphere conducive for student learning, teacher involvement and growth, community support and high expectations. What do these principals do in order to create such productive organizations? What strategies or special skills or abilities do these chief executive school officers possess that distinguish them from less able leaders?

A critical question that must be answered lies in the way in which principals create the atmosphere that stimulates these vital educational areas. Certainly, the principal's leadership style must be suited for the organizational context. This linkage is crucial. How often have we witnessed a principal who is effective in one organizational situation being terribly ineffectual in another? For example, a principal who possesses strong organizational skills, is task oriented and authoritative, may be extremely desirable in the context of a school with newly appointed teachers requiring specific directives and well-defined goals and objectives. In addition, if there are serious behavioral problems in the school and the community desires control and stability, a principal with a directive style would be duly suited for this setting. In this school site

1

example, the principal's style of directive leadership would be consonant with the school needs.

On the other hand, if a principal is appointed to a school that has a seasoned faculty with high professional standards and performance, a more appropriate leadership style would be of a collaborative type, consulting with faculty for shared decision making and goal setting. As indicated, the leadership style would be consonant with the organizational context.

But what undergirds any leadership style and ultimate management practice? When we alluded to the labels applied to the principal, for example, cultural leader, instructional manager, we identified leadership traits identified with a principal. But what does that actually mean? To be a skilled cultural leader, the principal must know about the school culture. The principal must be aware of the students, parents, faculty and staff. Demographic trends from a macro-organizational level are crucial in understanding growth patterns and emerging social groups, their needs and expectations. From a micro-organizational level, the principal who is a cultural leader would be better equipped to assist faculty and staff in working with students from divergent backgrounds. Sensitivity to these students in terms of language development and acquisition, communication nuances, family structure, and learning styles would be essential.

With respect to an effective organizational leader, the principal must be skilled in bureaucratic processes, time schedules, effective meeting techniques, room allocations, and transportation, in order to organize and maintain an efficient school enterprise. The efficient utilization of time affects student achievement, teacher performance and overall productivity. The literature clearly reflects 'time on task' activities, in which the students are engaged, as essential for maximizing student achievement. Teachers feel a greater sense of accomplishment when they perceive administrators supporting their 'teaching' time and avoiding scheduling unnecessary meetings and conferences. Of course, community members are also appreciative of schools that are managed well so that there is greater probability for student success.

In all these areas, we have indicated that the principal must be skilled in these processes and aware of the types of impact produced. How is this 'skill' developed? Is this an innate skill being a cultural leader? Is there an intuitive skill in being an organizational expert? We think not, although intuitive abilities are always helpful and can be distinctive in leaders. We believe that this skill is developed by having the appropriate and timely information available to principals in order for them to make sound decisions. When we examine the literature on decision making, we find many paradigms and theories, frameworks and models that suggest specific approaches. For example, Daniel Griffiths speaks of decision making in terms of: defining the problem; seeking information; considering alternatives; implementing the best approach; and evaluating the effectiveness of the approach (Griffiths, 1959). How 'real' is this decision-making approach in the context of the school setting? Do principals actually follow this step-by-step procedure? Do they have the time, knowledge and resources to enact this method? Recent research on decision making from the field suggests otherwise (Hallowitz and Dubin, in press). Indeed, if these models are not applicable, what does work? What do these 'effective' principals do? In the corporate context, do chief executive officers operate in this fashion? If we were to examine the skills and operating procedures of a chief executive officer in a corporate context, what comparisons could we draw between the corporate CEO and our effective principals?

Clearly, all effective administrators in either the corporate world or in the educational community make sound decisions. Sound decisions are made because administrators are aware of the necessary information flow upon which to make a decision, have access to it and in a timely manner. If critical information sources can be identified, channeled, interpreted and responded to methodically, systematically and preemptively, the 'skill' of the principal becomes real. If a principal knows where to look for information, is able to analyze it and apply it to various decisions, his school can function in more efficient and predictive ways.

Are effective principals aware of information flow sources? What types of 'systems' do they utilize in order to make effective decisions? How differently do they operate when compared to less effective principals? How differently do they operate when compared to chief executive officers in a corporate and larger scale environment? Would a principal, who is made aware of the information sources, given access to them through a systematized program on a computer, or short- and long-term systematic planning, be predictive and thus preemptive in addressing problems, avoid the pitfalls described earlier that arise between the leadership style and the organizational context? Consider the possibilities. If a principal had these skills, that is, an understanding of the information flow sources, had access to these in a programmed fashion that signalled potential problems based upon the information, principals could begin adapting leadership and decision-making styles in accordance with the school need.

In summation the three main components involved in effective decision making are:

identifying the various information sources in the school and how they interrelate;

having timely access to this information; and

systematizing the information process so that it can signal potential problems for preemptive decision making or at least provide relevant information to be utilized for planning and analysis.

This anthology examines effective decision-making practice by distinguished principals, chief executive officers, professors of educational administration and exemplary teachers. It also explores the various school operational functions and information sources that would be considered critical to identify and analyze in order to signal school problems.

Chapter 1 provides an overview of some of the more significant school reorganization efforts and how the locus of responsibility is shifting from the district to the local school site. Emphasis on the changing role of the principal from that of instructional leader to chief executive officer is explored.

The four sections in Chapter 2, written by award winning principals, represent various parts of the nation and different school levels (elementary, middle schools and high schools). Each provides a personalized systems information approach in preemptive decision making in various school operations. To provide for continuity and adherence to the central themes, the book's editor provided content and editorial guidance to each contributing author. The four principals (one to each of the four sections in Chapter 2) were nominated to the book's editor by their respective organizations, Elementary School Administrators Association and the Secondary Schools Principals Association, as meeting the following criteria advanced by the book's editor:

> demonstrated commitment to excellence for all children, that is, programs that have met the academic and social needs of all children as a school principal;
>
> contributed to the advancement of education, participation in community affairs, membership in relevant professional organizations;
>
> recognized amongst peers as leaders in their fields;
>
> received distinguished honors award by their professional organization.

Specifically, Chapter 2 focuses on: Pupil Attendance, Scheduling and Transportation; Personnel; The Effective Principal and the Curriculum; and Organizational Factors. As with all the sections, the *Key Points* will identify the critical elements of the chapter and be followed by discussion questions for student reflection and analysis.

In section one, Pupil Attendance, Scheduling and Transportation, Robert Ames illustrates how information impacts the decision-making process for the principal. Understanding the complex permutations of master scheduling, busing and transportation, maintenance, student behavior (on buses) as a means to anticipate potential areas of concern is important for effective early action on the part of the principal.

The second section in Chapter 2 stresses the area of personnel, credentialing, staffing, faculty load, salary, teaching responsibilities and evaluation. Its author, Bruce Bartlett, shows how understanding a principal's many constituencies, including faculty and staff, provides the information necessary to motivate faculty and staff and engender power and involvement. It also enables the principal to minimize the problems associated with unfair course assignments, evaluations, content area and inappropriate teaching. A case study will be provided to underscore this material.

A principal's knowledge of curriculum is crucial in assuming the role of instructional leader, one of the important functions of the principal/CEO. In section three, Caryl Burns furnishes a number of sources: state frameworks, feeder schools and their curricula, multicultural needs, and graduation requirements. This admix of data must be utilized by the principal if there is to be effective decision making at the school site. The interweave of curriculum analysis with scheduling and staffing will be the focus offered by Burns. A case study is also offered.

The fourth and final section comprising Chapter 2 deals with the larger composition of the school, that is, organizational factors. Since schools are open systems, they are subject to pressures that are often outside the decision-making domain of the principal. Demographic trends, parent/family histories, communication networks and assessment instruments all provide the type of data sources that could greatly facilitate effective decision making on the part of the principal. Knowing what to anticipate, as reflected in these trends and articulated by these various constituencies in a systematic way, lays the groundwork for future planning, in addition to signaling potential problems that could surface. All of these concerns are addressed thoroughly by its author, Susan Van Zant.

Chapter 3 focuses on the role of the principal as proactive decision maker and CEO from the viewpoint of four chief executive officers. How do they perceive the transfer of power bases from a centralized to a decentralized structure? What impact will it have on budget decisions, authority, personnel, at both the district and local levels? What impact will this have on the educational system? How does the business community view the effective/ineffective principal? What does the reform movement mean to chief executive officers representing different professional areas? These are some of the issues captured via interview format in Chapter 3.

In section one of Chapter 3, Robert Corrigan, President of San Francisco State University, shares his views as CEO on effective decision making and the education reform movement. In section two, we hear from Ramon Cortines, Superintendent of the San Francisco Unified School District and former Superintendent of the San Jose Unified and

Pasadena School Districts, providing the superintendent's perspectives. In section three, Jerry Hume, Chairman of the board and CEO at Basic American Foods, Inc., furnishes a corporate executive's perspective upon the role of a CEO and the significance of early decision making based on reliable current information. He also provides perspectives on our schools as they impact the business community. Finally, in section four, Henrietta Schwartz, Dean of the School of Education at San Francisco State University, contributes a university dean's CEO perspective on the role of the principal as a proactive decision maker.

Chapter 4 focuses on three important areas of proactive decision making: an analysis of an urban school organizational structure as it developed proactive decision strategies to deal with disciplinary and instructional issues at the site; the many types of computerized programs that can be incorporated into the principal's management system at the school site; and the social-psychological role the principal assumes in addressing the needs and concerns of faculty and staff in order to create and maintain a healthy working environment. These sections were written respectively by educational administration professors Emily Brizendine and Jake Perea, Hal Jonsson and Stanley Rothstein. I offer a final section on an innovative pedagogy called interactive video that develops decision-making skills. It involves the utilization of a computerized simulation that presents a case study with various consequences predicated on options selected. The process allows for students to engage in analyzing a given problem, select the appropriate decision and then get immediate feedback as to the consequences of that decision through the use of video simulated feedback. It is a new and exciting application which merges computerized technology with video.

Chapter 5 briefly provides the perspective of exemplary teachers as they share their views of effective proactive principals. They discuss their work environment, specific programs with which they have been involved and what they consider to be important characteristics of effective principals. These teachers were selected to write their respective sections as a result of their demonstrated commitment to the profession, achievement of awards and/or involvement in relevant programs. In addition, the editor feels that input of the men and women in the trenches, as it were, is essential since they are the ones most impacted by proactive and reactive decision making at the site level.

Finally, in Chapter 6 the conclusion provides a vision for, and ask questions about, the school organization and decision-making processes. Can schools be restructured and, if so, what new roles will teachers and principals assume? Will the use of information sources identified by the contributing authors be utilized in different ways in order for principals to be more proactive in their decision making? Will the education reform movement make a difference?

Reform, Restructuring and the Principal as Chief Executive Officer

Our educational system in the United States is charged with the companion capability of changing, improving and advancing our multicultural and ethnically diverse society while reflecting it and defining it in its present form. It is an extremely difficult undertaking. It is as though the educational system is a video film separated into a series of historical snapshots or slides representing the frozen part of a sequence of our culture at that instant in time. When the film is allowed to advance, it offers a view of the direction it is headed. There is an almost metaphysical quality to it. When at pause, it allows us to see us at the moment. This dual imaging is vitally important because we can understand our complex and evolving educational enterprise only thorugh the historical continuum.

Educational reform is upon us. It is vitally important for educators to assess this movement as to its impact on our schools and our society. What will these 'waves' of reform produce in the name of constructive change in the coming years? What analysis can be assigned to this reform movement from a historical perspective? How does this process of reform take place?

As articulated in the research document by Far West Laboratory, entitled *The Redesigning of Education: A Collection of Papers Concerned with Comprehensive Educational Reform*, the current wave of restructuring efforts represents a natural outgrowth of the excellence movement, which established a reform agenda consisting of general goals at which schools could aim (Far West Laboratory, 1988). While the emphasis was on what constituted effectiveness, there was less attention to how the goals could be reached. Restructuring efforts, on the other hand, tend to be concerned at least initially with creating structures, processes, and conditions for change (for example, establishing leadership teams, decentralizing, empowering teachers). As such, restructuring can be described as a logical and natural successor to the excellence movement.

Second, the problems faced by schools, especially those in urban settings, are enormous, some say paralyzing. Many urban educators have become convinced that the existing schooling patterns and practices will have to give way to new ones. Doing something about the achievement gap between minority and disadvantaged youngsters and their counterparts is now recognized by many as the most serious problem facing urban education.

Third, much has been said about the compatibility between our present educational system and the industrial age — an age we are moving away from. Now schools must be concerned with meeting the educational needs of the information-oriented age — an age that demands different competencies for leading productive and satisfying lives.

Fourth, *A Nation at Risk* (National Commission on Excellence in Education, 1988), and virtually every national report issued since, stresses the economic dangers facing the United States. A decline in economic productivity, vigorous challenges to America's long dominance of world markets, and economic growth no longer a 'given', are indicators of danger. Economic competitiveness has become a powerful challenge in goading the educational system toward improving its quality and relevance for a post-industrial society.

Finally, there have been major advances in basic research and applied technology that will significantly influence both learning and instruction. From cognitive psychology come different conceptions of how learners learn. Advances in computer technology (for example, information storage, retrieval, and manipulation, artificial intelligence) will permit very different types and levels of interaction between learners and a knowledge base.

These conditions contribute to a complicated problem mix and add urgency to educators' natural tendencies to want to improve the educational system. As a result, slow and steady improvement of the existing system is no longer seen by many as acceptable. Major change, restructuring, and redesign of that system are fast becoming the catchwords.

A Nation at Risk: The Imperative for Educational Reform, a report by the National Commission on Excellence in Education (1988), is regarded as being the impetus for the current reform movement in education. It assessed our schools as being deficient in producing the types of students and, ultimately, societal members (workers) who could effectively compete with other countries' students and workers, in the world marketplace. When comparing United States' student test results of 'average mathematics scores for students in the eighth grade, 1981–82' with students from other countries — Japan, Netherlands, France, Belgium, Hungary, British Columbia, Belgium (French), Ontario, Scotland, England and Wales, Finland, New Zealand and Sweden — the United States' students ranked thirteenth out of the fifteen countries cited (Walberg, 1986). Another test that compared the United States' students' performance with students from twelve other countries — Japan, Finland, Ontario, Sweden, Hungary, New Zealand, Belgium (Flemish), England and Wales, British Columbia, Belgium (French), and Scotland — dealing with algebra and calculus (twelfth graders), resulted in the United States ranking last.

The test results and others created a reflex reaction that produced a host of blue ribbon panels and reports alluded to in the introductory chapter that were charged with:

> analyzing our school system in order to determine why our students
> were not achieving greater skill levels;

making appropriate recommendations to correct the malaise and ineffectiveness that has overcome our school system;

developing new organizational structures that would better meet the demands of our high technology society in the world marketplace;

restructuring our schools to improve the overall decision-making process by 'professionalizing' the teaching occupation;

probing our training institutions in order to assess their effectiveness in producing quality programs and educators.

The following represents a distillation of the lists of recommendations from these various reports cited:

develop and utilize teacher leadership;

reduce class size;

make teacher salaries more competitive with other professions;

develop a new system of setting and enforcing professional teaching standards;

intervene in 'schools at risk';

initiate aggressive teacher recruitment campaigns;

develop professional development schools, analogous to teaching hospitals;

improve teacher subject knowledge content and pedagogical techniques;

provide more institutional 'space' and improve overall conditions (support system, decentralized decision making, resources) for educators;

develop more effective teacher assessment instruments.

These practical and well-documented recommendations emerged from the hundreds of surveys, interviews, and observations from experts and others in the field. Of course, an important aspect of information gathering focused on successful leadership, that is, what conditions these researchers found in evidence at schools that were considered effective.

The type of activity that has initially resulted from the volumes of reports and lists of recommendations generally has focused on State regulatory changes dealing with certification of teachers, more stringent curriculum and graduation requirements, increased homework assignments, strict disciplinary procedures and the like. There have been more regulations in the last few years emanating from State levels than the previous twenty years. Local school district administrators and teachers have been frustrated and enervated by these regulations and have seen very few positive, tangible results.

Many major school districts are beginning to realize that for a real reform in education to take place the emphasis is not to be on State regulations but on individual schools utilizing their own culture, community and special needs to restructure themselves, to redefine their role toward teaching and learning in a coordinated and systematic fashion. A significant organizational change cited in the aforementioned reform reports was decentralization. This would mean that the district office would encourage a significant expansion of local autonomous efforts. Already there is ample evidence that this is occurring. In a recent article in *Phi Delta Kappan*, the emphasis on local schools has been described succinctly: 'Policies designed to reform education are no better than schools that implement them. Therefore, the target of State policy must always be the individual school. Within schools the focus must be on organizational arrangements that maximize the organizational competence of the school' (Timar, 1989).

The following represents several school restructuring efforts already underway in several districts thorough out the country. We see this as a development that will continue and affect most school districts nationwide.

San Diego, California.

> Approximately thirty-five schools in this 117,000 student district are in the process of restructuring their programs making any changes necessary to improve student learning. Eventually, district leaders hope to provide all schools with greater flexibility and autonomy. Most of the literature on restructuring has been focused on the individual school as the locus of change (Olsen, 1989).

In San Diego it is recognized that teachers and principals at each site must be intimately involved in redesigning their programs and curriculum. At the same time the superintendent has decreed that to further school autonomy the district office must cease functioning as controllers and monitors of school sites. The superintendent has decided that

> The Central Office staff members who oversee these schools [the thirty-five mentioned above] and all 118 others in the district are expected to change. Instead of serving as the monitors and enforcers of district policy they are to become the enablers and facilitators (Olsen, 1989).

The central office 'should be a service center not a command post barking orders' (Kearns and Doyle, 1988).

As an example of San Diego placing emphasis on local school sites, the superintendent has ruled that no central office middle managers can reject an innovative plan proposed by a school. As one central office middle manager phrased it,

> Previously I could get up in front of principals and say 'This is what is required and this is the way you are required to implement it'. Now you think twice before you tell people what to do at a school site because there is a certain amount of power at the school (Kearns and Doyle, 1988).

Chicago, Illinois. The Chicago school system has been called the worst in the nation by former Secretary of Education, William Bennett. It has a drop-out rate of 45 per cent with half the city's high schools scoring on college entrance examinations at the bottom 1 per cent of the nation.

In an experiment scheduled to begin in the summer of 1989, Chicago will reduce the power of its central office by abolishing 1000 administrative jobs and turn control over to local schools. Each school will have the authority to decide how its budget is managed and what teachers it chooses to hire. An estimated forty million dollars that will be saved on cutting down the central office, is to be turned over to local schools. 'Who knows what will happen between now and then ... a very big step has been taken' (Snider, 1989).

Miami, Florida. Dade County, Florida, the nation's fourth largest school district with 260 schools and 225,000 students has not let its size stop it from implementing innovative school site management programs. Individual schools have been given unprecedented autonomy in staffing, budgetary and instructional decisions.

Rochester, New York. In a system with 33,000 students, sixty-eight per cent minority, one in three does not finish high school. Twenty per cent are absent at least one day a week. Among girls 15 to 19 years old, one in eight becomes pregnant each year or almost 1400 a year. Rochester is determined to end the failure of its schools. Again, the emphasis is on the school site. Teachers will receive up to $70,000 a year in salary which will rank them among the highest paid in the country. In addition to high salaries, each local school will be able to shape its curriculum, what is taught and how it is to be taught. Teachers and principals agreed to accept greater accountability and responsibility. One important element of change at the local school site is every teacher and principal will take personal responsibility for a group of twenty students for several years. District administrators feel that the local schools will feel more responsible and be more accountable by empowering teachers and principals, i.e., giving them a voice about the structure of the school and about what they teach (staff writer, *New York Times*, 1988).

The Council of Great City Schools met in the Fall of 1988 in Toledo, Ohio, with forty of the nation's largest urban districts represented by their superintendents and board members. The conference attendees were well aware of the need to reform teaching and administration in their districts. They called 'centralization' a pitfall that does not make educational sense. 'In some districts a teacher cannot rearrange seats in the classroom without committing an infraction of district policy' (Olsen, 1988). Several of the conference attendees have begun to experiment with decentralized decision making and school-based management.

William J. Hume, Chairman and Chief Executive Officer of Basic American Foods Corporation, is a member of the California Business Roundtable's Education Task Force which has been studying education in California and has issued a widely read and discussed report on reform and restructuring California Schools. In an editorial in the *San Francisco Chronicle* he writes:

Decentralizing the school system is one of the most exciting notions on the educational horizon and one of the six primary reform recommendations to come out of the California Business Roundtable's report *Restructuring California Education*. We can begin by giving those at the local level more responsibility for making decisions about how our children are educated and more tools to implement those decisions.

The State budget system should be simplified and decentralized with individual schools allowed to control their educational programs and be judges on the results they produce.... Only by creating a new structure that reorganizes social and economic realities while allowing teachers to teach students to learn and parents to participate will we be able to give our children the tools they will need to meet the economic challenges of the next century (Hume, 1989).

The reports on educational reform — The Carnegie Forum Report, The Holmes Group, The Commons Commission Report, *A Nation at Risk*, and *Restructuring California Education* — all have a central theme in common, that is, the school principal is to have more autonomy in decision making at the school site. This is reinforced by the restructuring begun in such major school districts as San Diego, Chicago, Miami and Rochester, described in the preceding pages. All of the restructuring transfers autonomy, responsibility and accountability to the school site. Obviously this means an expanded role for school principals and the empowering of the school administrators and teachers. What will this new role for the principal entail? A principal must be 'on top of' all events and the information flow of the school enterprise in order to effectively discharge this new and broader responsibility. There is a continuous flow of critical information at each school site which, if organized and directed appropriately through the use of a computerized system, could signal the school principal that there is a malfunction that requires administrative attention. This is the organizational process in industry and would serve extremely well within a school format. A preliminary study of school principals' decision making reveals that principals become aware of on-site problems through reports by teachers, parents, community sources, newspapers, students, and therefore appears to be reactive rather than proactive (Hallowitz and Dubin, in press). What needs to be explored is a corporate model of data identification and processing, and whether that model would enable a school principal to take the initiative rather than be inactive while the problems develop, increase and multiply.

There are different types of information at each school dealing with test scores, scheduling, absenteeism, training, transportation, purchasing, and maintenance. It is fragmented and unsystematic in most cases. It must be digested, analyzed for the principal with clearly indicated warning signals of abnormalities that portend brewing problems in a usable and timely fashion. This is what is envisioned by restructuring. Corporations increasingly have such computerized information systems in place in order for the chief executive officer to initiate action prior to a crisis developing.

We are on the verge of an exploding movement of decentralization and great responsibilty for the local school and its principal. The principal's role as instructional leader appears to be one component of a variety of essential roles. The principal is charged with control of all school functions and operations — truly the chief executive officer, who will need state-of-the-art technology to plan and decide, implement and monitor the many initiatives that must be undertaken in order to reform American education.

Key Points

1   Reform efforts have focused on State regulations thus further emphasizing centralization.

2 Some major districts are convinced that reform based on State regulation is not improving education and is moving towards local school autonomy and empowerment of principals and teachers.
3 This movement toward school responsibility and accountability is changing the role of the principal from Instructional Leader to Principal/Chief Executive Officer.
4 To effectively discharge this expanded role, the Principal/CEO needs a systematic information system, using technology in order to be in a position to be proactive rather than reactive in problem solving, decision making, implementation and monitoring.

Discussion Questions

1 What has been the history behind the education reform movement?
2 What impact will decentralization have on district level policy?
3 What staff development programs must be initiated to orient teachers and administrators to their new school bound roles?
4 How would you contrast this education reform movement with previous ones?
5 What would you anticipate the next education reform movement will focus on and when do you think it will occur?

Note

1 In a study currently under review it appears that computers are not being used for an information system that would provide data on abnormalities requiring early administrative intervention. Software needs to be created for this purpose.

Suggested Readings

THE CALIFORNIA COMMISSION ON THE TEACHING PROFESSION (1985) 'Who Will Teach Our Children', Dorman Commons, Chair, Sacramento, CA.
CARNEGIE FORUM ON EDUCATION AND THE ECONOMY'S TASK FORCE ON TEACHING AS A PROFESSION (1985) 'A Nation Prepared: Teachers for the 21st Century' (The Report of the Task Force on Teaching as a Profession), New York: Carnegie Corporation.
FAR WEST LABORATORY (1988) 'The Redesign of Education: A Collection of Papers Concerned with Comprehensive Educational Reform,' San Francisco, CA.

GRIFFITHS, D (1959) *Administrative Theory*, New York: Appleton Century Crafts, Inc.

GRIFFITHS, D. et al., (1987) *Leaders for America's Schools: The Report and Papers of the National Commission on Excellence in Educational Administration*, California: McCutchan Publishing Corporation.

HALLOWITZ, G. and DUBIN, A. (in press) *Decision-Making in Schools*.

THE HOLMES GROUP (1986) 'Tomorrow's Teachers: A Report of the Holmes Group', The Holmes Group. East Lansing, MI.

HUME, J. (1989) Editorial Page, *San Francisco Chronicle*, 1 April.

KEARNS, D.T. and DOYLE, D.P. (1988) *Winning the Brain Race: A Bold Plan To Make Our Schools Competitive*, San Francisco, CA: Institute for Contemporary Studies Press.

THE NATIONAL COMMISSION ON EXCELLENCE IN EDUCATIONAL ADMINISTRATION (1987) 'Leaders for America's Schools: The Report of the National Commission on Excellence in Educational Administration'.

THE NATIONAL COMMISSION ON EXCELLENCE IN EDUCATIONAL ADMINISTRATION (1988) *A Nation of Risk*.

OLSEN, L. (1988) 'The Restructuring Puzzle', *Education Week*, pp. 9–15.

OLSEN, L. (1989) 'In San Diego, Managers Forging "Service" Role', *Education Week*, pp. 15–18.

SNIDER, W. (1989) 'Chicago's "Summit": A Populist Blueprint To Reshape Schools', *Education Week*, pp. 25–8.

TIMAR, T. (1989) 'The Politics of School Restructuring', *Phi Delta Kappan*, Dec., pp. 266–275.

WALBERG, H.J. (1986) 'What Works in a Nation Still At Risk.'*Educational Leadership*, 15 September, pp. 7–10.

Chapter 2

Proactive Decision Making: Perspectives from Award Winning Principals

Introduction

The following chapters represent the reflections of four successful principals, articulated by them candidly and personally. The information they present and the style in which they present it are indicative of their unique and distinctive administrative approaches and demonstrate an understanding and application of effective practices. They all approach their contribution to this anthology with their own sense of what management and supervision means. They focus on curriculum, personnel, scheduling and the school organization, all vital aspects of all schools. Throughout their descriptions of their respective operations and approaches, the thread that connects their strategies and efforts is their sense of the larger context, the bigger picture. Within this macro-orientation and structure, they also identify the constituent groups or individuals whose contributions will be meaningful and substantive within the context of that specific area or decision. The group that contributes to effective decision making and those most impacted by those decisions are those involved by these principals. They practice administrative strategies that utilize appropriate personnel with context-specific expertise for input in decision making, ascertain the needs of the various constituent groups effected by those decisions and then assess the impact of the procedures and plans.

Robert Ames presents his administrative duties from a distinctly pragmatic vantage point, clearly identifying those areas vitally important for effective school operations. He provides extremely useful information regarding scheduling, attendance, program development and transportation that can almost be used as a functional guide to review school operations.

Bruce Bartlett indicates in his opening remarks the need for ownership from his staff regarding the hiring process. The most significant means by which faculty/staff develop a real commitment to the process is to include them in the decision-making efforts. In this case they constitute both decision-making experts and those who would be affected by those decisions since they would be working closely with those newly-hired teachers in the years to come.

It is clear from Caryl Burns' well researched and documented contribution on curriculum that effective principals need to be cognizant of curriculum as it is mandated by various local, state or national agencies, as it impacts teachers, and how it is perceived by students. Again, she is clear to perceive the organizational process both from the standpoint of the total system as well as its parts.

Susan Van Zant captures this macro-organizational perspective quite well as she identifies the myriad of school related factors that impact the system. The committees, events, programs, activities, awards, and ceremonies that are identified and initiated by the administration in order to meet specific school needs are extremely orienting and, as well, enlightening. It is clear how stimulating these efforts can and have been in creating the kind of unity and common purpose necessary for effective school direction and management. In addition, what underlie these administrative efforts are the identification and utilization of appropriate information sources crucial for effective school practices.

Section One: Pupil Attendance, Scheduling and Transportation
Robert L. Ames
Naches Valley High School, Washington

Community involvement, student centered emphasis and curriculum development are three major areas that Ames has focused his considerable energies and talents developing at Naches Valley High School for the past ten years. He has been President of the Association of Washington School Principals and most recently been actively involved in developing Vision 2001, the comprehensive review of the direction of education for the state of Washington. One important component of this comprehensive program involves community learning, that is, parents learn about how they can provide guidance and support for their children and upgrade their own academic skills and professional pursuits. Ames received his Bachelor of Science from the University of Idaho and his Master in Education from Central Washington University.

Pupil Attendance

Student attendance and lateness can be a difficult problem if you allow it be. Regardless of the size of the school, an effective attendance policy and practice should and can be enforced. It takes a strong commitment by the principal, faculty and staff involved. We, at Naches Valley High School, initiated several changes over the last ten years to ensure that our attendance works in a positive atmosphere, with the staff, administration and community.

Academic attendance regulations

Laws of the State of Washington specify that the parents have the primary responsibility for insuring the attendance of their children at school. They further state that the students shall be regular and punctual in their attendance. The attendance procedure at Naches Valley High School is designed to assist parents to carry out this responsibility, to help the pupil recognize the importance of regular and prompt school attendance as it relates to school progress, to understand the world of work and to promote the safety of pupils by knowing of the student's whereabouts during the school day through reasonable school procedures.

In keeping with the academic atmosphere of Naches Valley High School, attendance in class is an essential part of the total classroom and learning experience. In emphasizing the importance of this area, teachers consider student attendance in their grading system. Extended absence due to illness or personal circumstance is dealt with on an individual basis at the request of the student or the parents. All requests for review are directed to the principal.

Effects of daily attendance on final grades

Attendance accounts for 20 per cent of a student's final grade during each grading period. The other 80 per cent of the grade is determined by factors such as class participation, academic work and testing, as determined by the individual teacher.

As a means of instilling values of responsibility and personal accountability, students whose absences are not excused, experience the natural consequences of their truancy. They are not permitted to make up missed work assignments, and any graded activities which occur during the truancy are graded as if the student had chosen not to participate in them.

Excused absences are verified by the parent or school authority who can explain and/or justify the absence. When a student returns to school or class after the absence, a note explaining the student's absence, signed by a parent or guardian is presented to the office. Dental or doctor appointment cards serve to verify the appointment and are presented to the school prior to the appointment. The student will be given an absence card to take to each teacher to sign. This card is left with the last period teacher who will send it to the office.

Procedure

1 Students are expected to attend all assigned classes each day. Teachers will keep a record of absence and tardiness.

2 Teachers will send a list of absentees to the office 2nd period, and an absence list will be compiled and made available for reference. This is the official absence list for the State reports.

3 Teachers will inform students at the beginning of the course that each absence or tardiness will contribute to a possible loss of credit for the course (three tardies count as one absence and students will be assigned detention immediately).

4 Students may be withdrawn from a class and lose a credit for that class upon compiling ten absences.

5 Students may be withdrawn from school for the trimester when compiling ten full absences.

6 When a student returns to school, following each absence, he is to present a note, signed by his parent, indicating the reason for the absence and then record that information on the student attendance card in the office with his signature. All students must sign in regardless of the reason for being absent.

7 When a student has been absent five times from a teacher's class, the teacher contacts the parents by either phone or mail. After eight absences, the teacher will again contact the parents. On or before the tenth absence, the teacher will contact the office informing them of previous parent contacts and requests a parent conference to be held.

8 After the parent conference, the teacher or teachers involved will make a recommendation as to whether or not the student should be withdrawn from class.

9 In the event a student is withdrawn from more than one class in a trimester for attendance reasons, he may be withdrawn from all classes.

10 Any student who has been denied credit in class for failure to meet attendance requirements may appeal that decision by requesting a formal review of his record. This will be done by making a request in writing to the principal asking for a Review Board on attendance. The review board will consist of the counselor, teachers involved, and the principal or his designee. The student and his parent will be required to attend the review board session. It is possible that credit may be reinstated if the student's performance in class has been satisfactory.

11 Absences resulting from work, family vacations, apple picking, hunting, and other matters will be considered excused only when arrangements have been made and approved prior to the absence. A student must obtain a pre-arranged absence request form from the office. This form must be signed by parents and

teachers and turned in to the office before the absence occurs; however, attendance grade will be affected.

12 School related absences: field trips, special programs, etc., sometimes result in class absences. Faculty members responsible for initiating the activity are to notify other teachers prior to the absence. The student's responsibility is to make arrangements with his teachers for work that will be missed. These absences will be considered school related and attendance grades will not be affected.

Being late to class not only interferes with the education of the student who is tardy, but also the education of others in that class. For this reason every effort will be made to encourage punctual attendance at all classes. On this regard teachers and administrators may:

discuss the problem with the student;

contact and discuss the problem with parents;

require that extra time be made up;

require extra assignments;

take other reasonable preventative action; or

pursue more stringent disciplinary action which may include suspension.

The above policy on truancy is intended as a guide to be followed in the majority of cases. Teachers or administrators may impose other reasonable punishment if it is intended to correct the behavior of the student. With this attendance policy and administration commitment to attendance, our daily absenteeism has averaged four per cent a day for the past five years. Prior to this proactive attendance policy, absenteeism averaged ten to twelve per cent in 1980.

Student grading policy

94 –	100	= A
86 –	93	= B
77 –	85	= C
70 –	76	= D
69 –	Below	= F

Performance class

20% Attendance (60 of 60 days)	100.0
20% Participation (58 of 60 days)	96.0
20% Quizzes Average	60.3
20% Skills	49.4
20% Project	55.0
	5⟌360.7
	72.1 or 'D' grade

Academic class

20% Attendance (53–60 days)	88.0
20% Unit Tests	95.4
20% Quizzes (4–6) (2 average)	96.0
20% Participation	94.3
20% Major Paper	96.0

$$5\overline{)469.7}$$

<u>93.9</u> or 'B' grade

Daily attendance percentages

Number of Days	Absentee percentage
0 –	100%
1 –	98% (59 of 60 days)
2 –	96% (58 of 60 days)
3 –	95%
4 –	93%
5 –	91%
6 –	90%
7 –	88%
8 –	86%
9 –	85%
10 –	83%

Pro rata incoming or transferring students' attendance according to number of days remaining in trimester.

Areas of focus

First and foremost, it is important for the principal to work in the attendance office in the morning. His presence projects a strong commitment to this value system. The students must know that if they were absent they will be accountable.

Second, we have incorporated attendance into our grading system. The students understand that they can positively affect their grade by responsibly attending class.

Third, we have color coded attendance slips for staff so that a school or medical excuse, and/or a truancy can be easily discerned. These were also designed with community input so that students were not punished when it was impossible for them to atend school for a short period of time.

Fourth, pre-arranged absentee forms are required by the students to fill out and turn into the office before they leave on a trip; with family, college institutions, field trips, etc.

Fifth, students who need to leave school early during the day for appointments must get an early dismissal slip from the office before school and sign-out before leaving campus.

Sixth, we call each student's home who is on the attendance list every day. All the calls home to parents and/or their work place are done by 10.30 a.m.

Seventh, students who are late to class three times are assessed one absence.

Master Schedule

One of the most difficult problem areas from year to year, whether in a large or small school, is building the master schedule. There are so many variables that affect this process that in a small school district it can become a nightmare. The basic problems are school funding by the state legislature, additional requirements for graduation, teacher endorsement areas, students' incoming and outgoing population, migrant and college entrance requirements. All these important areas that impact scheduling have made us all try different types of models ranging from six to eight period days.

Building the master schedule to provide students the number of classes needed to meet graduation requirements and at the same time offer the faculty the class size and space to accomplish this goal is the primary task. In order to do this, there are three important philosophical and practical approaches we employ at Naches Valley High School:

First: We, as a school district, focus actions on helping children and students at risk by:
providing educational programs for our students in poverty and at risk.

Second: Increasing the level of student performance by:
increasing the use of advance technology in schools for teachers and students;
reaching out and bringing parents into schools as partners in education of their children;
using student tutors and mentors for assisting their fellow students who need special help;
practicing the belief that all kids can learn and raise the level of expectations for all students.

Third: Increasing the teachers' knowledge in their subject areas through professional sponsored workshops:
hiring professional talented teachers;
recruiting business persons as guest speakers and lecturers.

Andrew E. Dubin

These are some of the major ideas and visions that provide the foundation for developing a master schedule. Of course, the district financial (enrollment) status does affect the number of course sections we are able to offer our students. Nonetheless, our intent is to find new and better ways of assessing what students need to know, and impart that knowledge in a way that will be useful and meaningful in their lives.

Summary sheet
Naches Valley High School is a comprehensive high school. The school was built in 1980 to accommodate 500 students. Our present enrollment is 390, with twenty-two full-time staff and three shared with our middle school.

I have a full-time librarian, counselor, and vice-principal/athletic director. The school was planned well to meet the teachers' needs to deliver instruction in all areas. As you can see by our course offerings we are able to provide a very balanced, but challenging curriculum to our students, and supplies and materials to meet the designed course content. With our seven period school day the faculty sees on the average of twenty students each period.

Language Arts	Curriculum	Number of Sections
Courses required to graduate from NVHS		
*English 9	1	4
*English 10	1	4
English 9/10	1	1
*English 11	1	4
*English 12	1	3
Annual	1	1
Journalism	1	1
Applied Communications	1	2
	8	

Science		
*Biology	1	4
*Physical Science	1	4
Geology	1	1
Chemistry	1	1
Physics	1	1
Agriculture Science	1	1
Honors Biology	1	1
Honors Chemistry	1	1
	8	

Math (2 of the below)

Applied Math	1	1
General Math	1	1
Algebra	1	2
Algebra 2	1	3
Trig./Limits	1	1
Geometry	1	3
Calculus	1	1
Accounting	1	1
Electronic Math	1	1
Elective Math	1	1
Senior Math	1	1
	11	

Social Studies

*Washington State History/		
Career Education	1	5
*World History	1	4
*US History	1	4
*Contemp. World Problems	1	4
Asian Studies	1	1
	5	

Fine Arts (1 of the below)

Art 1	1	2
Art 2, 3, 4	1	2
Band	1	1
Choir	1	1
Images in Art	1	1
Drama	1	1
Photography	1	1
	7	

Practical Arts (1 of the below)

Woodshop 1	1	2
Advanced Woodshop	1	1
Construction Related	1	1
Keyboarding	1	3
General Shop	1	1
Computer Applications	1	1
Home Economics I	1	3
Home Economics II	1	1
Agriculture 1	1	1
Advanced metals	1	2
Advanced Agriculture	1	1
	11	

Foreign Language

Spanish I	1	3
Spanish II	1	2
French II	1	1
	3	

Physical Education

*PE 9	1	3
*PE 10/11/12	1	2
	2	

Computer Education

Computers	1	4

Transportation

Transportation plays an important role when developing a master schedule. Since we are one of the largest transportant districts in the state, the bus schedules are stable with little flexibility. Our school day starts at 8.15 a.m. and ends at 3.05 p.m. This gives us seven periods a day, fifty minutes long. Since we are a rural school district, approximately 65 per cent of our students ride the bus each day. At least 5 per cent of those students are on the bus two hours or more a day. Because we cover approximately 1000 miles with our eleven buses, we must have students from grades K–12 on the same bus. This causes some minor behavior problems, to say the least. If students wish to drive to school they know that being late is not excused. Our policy is that we run buses for their convenience, so they have the option of riding them or finding other means of transportation in order to arrive at school on time.

Students have designated pick-up points. They get on and off the bus there. The drivers are instructed not to let them off anywhere else unless they have permission from a school official. We transport students to school on the bus starting one-half mile from school.

Along with the eleven buses on route each day, we have six other ones to be used as spares, usually when regular buses break down, field trips are scheduled, band trips are scheduled, athletic events are scheduled. Most of these events are during or after school. Most of the school time activities are for the middle school.

Recently we purchased five new school buses, and plan to add one every three years, so our fleet is in good shape. Our transportation supervisor has maintenance done on each bus every 1300 miles and oil changes at 4500 miles. Our repairs have been minimal since the new buses have automatic transmissions. Previously, we were replacing clutches on buses at least once a year and some twice a year.

The following represents a sample of the entire inventory of vehicles:

District vehicle inventory

District Vehicle No.	Year	Make	Type
1	1988	Thomas	Bus
2	1978	Gillig	Bus
3	1970	Gillig	Bus
4	1972	Gillig	Bus
5	1967	Gillig	Bus
6	1974	Gillig	Bus
7	1975	Gillig	Bus
8	1988	Thomas	Bus
9	1977	Gillig	Bus
10	1976	Gillig	Bus
11	1981	Wayne	Bus
12	1988	Thomas	Bus
13	1984	Blue Bird	Bus
14	1986	Thomas	Bus
15	1988	Thomas	Bus
16	1988	Thomas	Bus
17	1979	Gillig	Bus
18	1945	Jeep	Jeep
19	1968	Ford	Car
20	1958	GMC	Dump truck
21	1972	Dodge	Van
22	1941	Grundig	Fork lift
23	1970	Dodge	3/4 ton p/u
24	1970	Dodge	1/2 ton p/u
25	1967	Ford	Car
26	1970	Dodge	1/2 ton p/u
27	1970	Dodge	1/2 ton p/u
28	1945	Jeep	Jeep
29	1965	Massey Ferguson	Tractor
30	1972	Dodge	3/4 ton 4x4p/u
31	1966	Chevrolet	Car
32	1982	Ford Courier	p/u
33	1982	Pontiac	Car
34	1987	Chevrolet	Station wagon

Rules and regulations for riding a school bus

These rules and regulations were prepared by the State Superintendent of Public Instruction with the advice of the Chief of the Washington State Patrol and the Director of Highways of the State of Washington, the Naches Valley School District and apply to all public school buses operating in the State of Washington.

The vehicle driver has authority and responsibility for the behavior of students using school district transportation. Students conduct themselves in accordance with the following rules and regulations. The right to use school district transportation may be denied to a student who violates these rules and regulations:

1　Students must never approach a bus until it has come to a complete stop and access doors have been opened.
2　Students shall cross the roadway only when the driver gives approval and the crossing must be only in front of and never behind the bus.
3　A student shall not be allowed to depart the vehicle other than at his or her boarding or alighting place unless permission is first obtained from the school Superintendent or designee.
4　Articles which may be hazardous in and of themselves which could cause injury to passengers shall not be transported in the passenger area of any school vehicle. The driver shall determine which articles are hazardous and are not to be transported in the passenger area of the vehicles.
5　Except for seeing eye dogs, no animal, reptile, fish or fowl is permitted on district vehicles.
6　Students shall not be allowed to stand when the vehicle is in motion (WAC 392–145–010).
7　Each pupil may be assigned a seat in which he will be seated at all times, unless permission to change is given by the school principal and/or driver.
8　Windows may be opened only with permission of the driver and when opened, no student shall extend any part of his or her body beyond the window ledge.
9　Pupils are to assist in keeping the bus clean by keeping their waste paper off the floor. Pupils must also refrain from throwing refuse out of the windows.

Key Points

1　School structure and adherence to clearly delineated procedure is highly important for the entire school community.
2　Reinforcement and follow-through regarding disciplinary procedure must be maintained. This can be done humanely without the traditional impersonal and damaging effect.
3　Acceptable social behavior, attitudes and mores are involved in the school mission and transmitted to the entire school community.

Discussion Questions

1   How is transportation scheduling integrated into master scheduling?
2   What are the advantages and disadvantages of scheduling six subject per days; seven subjects per day, etc., in terms of effective pedagogy?
3   What problems are present in a rural school environment that are unique?
4   What problems are present in a rural school environment that would cross-over into an urban or suburban setting?
5   How do you envision the education reform movement impacting the rural setting?

Section Two: Personnel
Bruce F. Bartlett
Cotton Creek Elementary School, Colorado

'Educational excellence' says Bruce Bartlett, 'is a process of becoming — of never being totally satisfied that we have done all that we can...' Guided by the belief that this means thoughtful change, experimentation, and risk taking, Bartlett created a peer-coaching project for his entire staff. Not only did this improve instruction, but it united the staff and created a more powerful school program. One of twenty five schools participating in a national thinking skills consortium, Shepardson has developed a model program for the teaching of thinking skills that Bartlett believes will improve test scores and reduce social conflicts. Bartlett began his career in education as a teacher in 1967 after receiving a BS at Eastern Michigan University. He holds an MEd and a PhD from Colorado State University.

The issue of personnel leadership and management is one of the most critical matters facing school administrators. From the perspective of the principal, a properly motivated and prepared staff means the achievement of instructional goals for students and a dynamic planning process for the continual improvement of staff and students. From the perspective of a teacher, personnel issues at the building level means having high quality colleagues to work with, opportunities for professional growth and improvement, and a positive climate for instruction. This includes a personal sense of self-worth and a feeling that your efforts are really making a difference.

'Site-based management' has recently received a great deal of attention. The term is generally used to describe a philosophy of management and leadership which decentralizes responsible decision making. The school-site level becomes the locus of decision making rather than the district level. In this way the decisions are closest to the customer. This philosophy of management is touted as being essential to maximize the instructional program for students. It provides for much more involvement by staff members in the design, implementation and evaluation of programs for students. It also increases staff development activities for the professional improvement of the faculty.

This higher level of involvement in decision making includes teachers in the screening, interviewing and selection of their potential colleagues. The procedure of using teams of teachers to help select other staff members creates some interesting and enigmatic situations. One advantage of utilizing teacher teams in the selection process is that it is well organized and prepared, and can allow each applicant to be more broadly represented. The interview, although orchestrated by one person (not necessarily the principal), can be structured so that each person on the committee can look in depth at one particular component of each applicant: related experiences in and out of the field; academic preparation; curriculum knowledge in a particular field; flexibility; human relations skills; and knowledge of current issues in education. The use of a team or comittee also tends to diminish the effect of any bias which might be held by any particular person, including the principal.

Another advantage of using a team or committee is that it assumes ownership of that candidate. The team feels a sense of responsibility for the future success of the applicant, should he ultimately be hired. Recently, we used a committee of primary teachers to assist in the screening, interviewing, and selection of a primary grades teacher. This team was actually interviewing and selecting someone who would be a colleague. Prior to the screening process we, the committee, determined the attributes thought important for the candidate to possess. After screening the files of propective applicants, we selected nine. The selection of these nine applicants, proved to be extremely difficult for two committee members. They were the most adamant in their beliefs that all the prescribed attributes be discernible in the paper screening process. The other team members felt differently and finally convinced them that the top group of applicant files would likely contain someone or several persons with those attributes even though they were not readily discernible in the initial paper.

The actual interviews were structured so that in the screening process, the committee members were to ask questions which pertained to their specific areas of expertise. Before the interviews began, I asked each committee member to be prepared to provide me a non-prioritized list of the three best applicants after the interviews were concluded. When the interviews finished and the lists of the three top applicants were handed in to me, two applicants appeared on nearly all lists while one person appeared on each list. I then made a series of reference checks on these top two applicants and the results confirmed our collective judgment that both applicants were excellent. The committee was then re-convened and asked, 'Who of these two excellent applicants would you most like to have as your own child's teacher?' As it turned out, we chose an excellent staff member.

In subsequent weeks, however, our newest colleague did have a few problems with students and parents. The problems were varied and not unlike the usual difficulties encountered by a person new to a community and school system. The difference, however, as I perceived it, was the way in which these problems were resolved. In all of my many years in education I have never witnessed the level of commitment and help on the part of fellow primary teachers. My perception is that the process of selection of their new team member had caused the other teachers to feel more responsible for her success. They spent, on many occasions, days of thier own time during the first semester, meeting with her and outlining plans to resolve the difficulties she was experiencing. In my opinion, this resulted from the selection committee's involvement in the hiring process.

Another interesting outcome that is created by staff members' participation in the process of screening, interviewing and recommending applicants, deals with 'favoritism.' This is caused when someone on the staff has a friend or a favorite applicant they believe would, 'clearly be the best person for the job.'

Case Study

A few years ago we were trying to find a fifth primary teacher. The team members involved were the other four primary teachers, my administrative assistant and myself. As we began the initial screening of applicant files for this position, one of the primary teachers began extolling the virtues of her friend. She acted like the applicant's press agent. In fact, one of the other teachers remarked sarcastically, 'We really don't need to interview anyone else'. The screening process continued and we did find several other excellent candidates for whom we scheduled interviews.

During the interview process, the 'friend' did a reasonable job answering the questions. At the end of her interview, though, she asked if we thought that her friendship with one of the team members would affect her chances of being selected. We indicated that our intention was to find the best person for the position regardless of their previous relationships.

Fortunately, several of the other applicants who were interviewed did outstanding jobs responding to our questions. They in turn had excellent questions for us. Even though these applicants seemed to be more qualified candidates than the 'friend', two different team members informed me that the team member was still maintaining support for her 'friend'. After all of the interviews were completed, I again asked the interviewers to submit to me a non-prioritized list of their three top choices. One list had the 'friend's' name on it. Two other applicants were on everyone's list. At that time I pulled that staff member aside. I explained the circumstances to her. I suggested that for her to support her friend at this point would damage her relationships with her colleagues and affect her credibility as a teaching professional. The teacher understood and agreed to support the wishes of the other team members. She also advised her friend that another applicant had been very impressive to the other team members and was considered to be the best candidate.

Finally, site-based decision making as it pertains to screening, interviewing and selecting teachers is especially difficult when it involves making a change in direction or philosophy for a particular grade or department. Very often the change which is needed is not perceived by the staff members in that grade or department. If they do recognize the need for the change, a principal should consider himself very fortunate. Assuming that the needed change can be accomplished much more readily from within, the necessity of having a person who agrees is extremely important. Therefore, when a principal has an opportunity to hire someone, it is important to find the most qualified person and one who can move the department in a certain direction.

With this as a backdrop, when a teacher needed to be hired by a committee of teachers who would represent a 'change agent', the following strategies were employed. Before the screening of files was begun, the team was called together. I explained my reason in suggesting that a new direction was needed and that my intention was to find a person with an appropriate background. I also rationalized my reasons for such a change. I said that my interest in a new direction was not triggered by any perceived weakness or lack of staff performance. Rather the decision-making team effort our school was moving toward required more assertive, experienced personnel, thus the need to find this type of person. I asked each team member to join me in this effort and to help me to find a staff member who could help to lead us in this new direction.

As a general rule, most of the pitfalls of selecting staff members in a site-based system where a high level of involvement is expected can be avoided by establishing the process by which the desired characteristics of a person are chosen before the process begins. It should be noted that many of the more traditional struggles regarding personnel matters which principals have typically faced are more easily resolved within the framework of this shared decision-making model.

Traditionally, a principal has had the responsibility of keeping a balance of experienced and inexperienced staff members in order to create a continual flow of new ideas and excitement, as well as a sense of stability and tradition. This balancing act has been a difficult one due to the number of candidates available to teach at certain positions. Within the framework of shared decision making and site-based management, the issue of balancing experienced faculty with inexperienced faculty is handled 'up front'. In fact, very often faculty members themselves bring up the issue during the discussion of the characteristics which would be desirable in prospective colleagues.

Ethnicity and gender are two other topics that draw much attention when a new staff member is to be hired. The law is very specific regarding hiring practices which might be considered discriminatory. Every effort must be made to insure that an appropriate balance of under-represented groups are present on the staff. This development and maintenance of 'balance' is also easier to accomplish in a site-based system. Issues of bias, bigotry, and/or nepotism are less likely to occur when the responsibility for hiring is shared with a number of professionals.

A site-based system of management also resolves other controversial issues such as class load. This issue alone is often the subject of controversy in elementary schools between classroom teachers and special area teachers. It is often a problem in secondary schools in departments with elective and non-elective courses. In a site-based system, these issues are confronted and discussed openly each semester by all faculty members or department chair persons and the principal. Even though it may be naive to assume that open discussion of such a sensitive issue will lead to complete resolution and happiness for each staff member, it does allow for potential understanding of the rationale behind any decisions impacting the class load of individual teachers.

The evaluation of faculty and staff is another pressing issue. Clearly no school district anywhere claims to have the perfect system. Differences of opinion regarding evaluation often result from the evaluation process. Under most conditions and in most school districts there is a prescribed cycle for the evaluation of teachers. For example, tenured teachers will receive a minimum of one formal evaluation every two to three years. Non-tenured teachers will receive a minimum of one formal written evaluation each year until they receive tenure status. Even though there is great diversity between districts, successful evaluation systems have many factors in common, whether they are used for tenured or non-tenured staff. These systems usually include a written set of minimal expectations and method of both formative and summative assessment, which are tied to the achievement of school and district goals, and a plan for staff development. The following is a sample list of minimum expectations as proposed by Tom McGreal from the University of Illinois, and a delineation of the differences between formative and summative performance appraised by Richard P. Manatt:

Statement of Minimum Expectations

1 Meets and instructs the students in the location at the time designated.

2 Develops and maintains a classroom environment conducive to effective learning within the limits of the resources provided by the district.

3 Prepares for classes assigned, and shows written evidence of preparation upon request of immediate supervisor.

4 Encourages students to set and maintain high standards of classroom behavior.

5 Provides an effective program of instruction in accordance with the physical limitations of the location provided and the needs and capabilities of the individuals or student groups involved.

6 Strives to implement by instruction the district's philosophy of education and to meet instructional goals and objectives.

7 Takes all necessary and reasonable precautions to protect students, equipment, materials and facilities.

8 Maintains records as required by law, district policy and administrative regulations.

9 Makes provisions for being available to students and parents for education related purposes outside the instructional day when necessary and under reasonable terms.

10 Assists in upholding and enforcing school rules and administrative regulations.

11 Attends and participates in faculty and department meetings.

12 Cooperates with other members of the staff in planning instructional goals, objectives and methods.

13 Assists in the selection of books, equipment and other instructional materials.

14 Works to establish and maintain open lines of communication with students, parents and colleagues concerning both the academic and behavioral progress of all students.

15 Establishes and maintains cooperative professional relationships with others.

16 Performs related duties as assigned by the administration in accordance with district policies and practices.

How Formative Evaluation Differs From Summative Evaluation in Performance Appraisal of the Education Professional

FORMATIVE		SUMMATIVE
To help teachers teach better (ongoing, descriptive, developmental, nonjudgmental)		To help management make better decisions (final, judgmental, comparative, adjudicative)
	Philosophy	
Each individual strives for excellence		Individuals achieve excellence only if supervised or evaluated by others
	Theory	
Evaluation is done to improve performance of the individual; reward or punishment is internal (learning theory)		Evaluation is done to improve the school organization and/or society; reward or punishment should be done externally (testing theory)
	Practice	
Evaluate the process of instruction, not the person 'coaching'		Evaluate the products of instruction as well as the process and the person, 'comparing and sorting'
	Focus	
Bottom up, holistic, free, serve me, for me		Top down, analytic, serve all stakeholders, for mutual benefit
	Appraiser	
A team approach, renewal		The first-line supervisor, accountability
	Continuum	
Clinical supervision	Professional evaluation	Weed out (bureaucratic evaluation)

The staff development component of the plan for staff evaluation usually is born out of the summative side of the evaluation model due to its ongoing, descriptive and non-judgmental nature. The basic thrust of the summative side of the evaluation/appraisal is renewal and improvement.

With the advent of strategic planning, school improvement teams and increased accountability, staff development has been more focused on the needs of each school site and its plans for achieving its goals. These plans, drawn up by parent, teacher and principal teams, have, as a necessary element for their success, a staff development component. Because of the importance of the success of each school's plan, staff development and training must be carefully planned and facilitated by the principal and the staff development personnel. In the initial stages of developing a school plan, no matter which model is used, a sense of collective focus on the mission and purpose of the school is necessary.

This sense of purpose becomes the driving force for planning staff development. Opportunities for staff development and training are difficult to implement when a school improvement plan is not in place and understood by the staff. This focused approach to training virtually eliminates the haphazard shotgun approach to staff development which has been common in the past. The problems traditionally created by the random approach have been: lack of focus on a particular school's needs, goals and issues; uneven distribution of staff development resources and animosity among staff members who perceive the uneven distribution of funds as preferential treatment for some staff members. By using the unified focus and the goals of the school as the driving force for staff development we are able to make much better use of our limited resources.

Case Study

Staff development, while providing one important aspect in the achievement of school goals, has also created some antagonism among staff members. One incident several years ago involved a team of staff members who had the opportunity to attend a workshop with Madeline Hunter at UCLA. The people who went, representing different grade levels, were self selected and needed to improve their instructional delivery systems. One of the charges to this group was to assist the principal by sharing with other staff members the 'elements of instruction' training which they were to receive. Upon their return from the first training sessions, rather than 'sharing' the information they learned from the workshops to their colleagues, they behaved condescendingly and offered little feedback. This created considerable tension. However, on a positive note, it did create impetus for the other reluctant faculty members to become more committed to the staff development process. In fact, they attended the next available workshop.

In summary, the personnel issues at the site level are pivotal to the success of any program. Site-based management, team shared decision making and the total sense of 'ownership' by faculty, community, and staff are the foundations for an effective school.

Key Points

1 Shared decision making extends the power base of the principal.
2 Shared decision making develops leadership skills in faculty members.
3 The proactive decision maker develops requisite skills in his staff prior to employing them in decision-making situations.

4 Shared decision making diffuses potential problems related to staff selection, development and budget allocation.
5 Open communication between the principal and faculty is a vital information source.

Discussion Questions

1 In the process of hiring teachers, what orientation program is necessary to prepare the hiring committee to perform its task effectively?
2 What advantages are there in autocratic decision making?
3 Should every principal utilize shared decision making in all instances?
4 How can technology be utilized in reviewing teacher applicants?
5 What are the legal ramifications involved in 'nepotism'?

Suggested Readings

AMBROSIE, F. and HALEY, P.W. (1988) 'The changing school climate and teacher professionalism', *NASSP Bulletin*, **72**, pp. 82–9.
BARTH, R.S. (1986) 'On sheep and goats and school reform', *Phi Delta Kappan* **68**, 4, pp. 293–6.
BOYER, E.L. (1988) 'School reform: Completing the course', *NASSP Bulletin* **72**, pp. 61–8.
DWYER, D.C., LEE, G.V., ROWAN, B. and BOSSERT, S. (1983) *Five Principals in Action: Perspectives on Instructional Management*, San Francisco, Far West Laboratory.
LIEBERMAN, A. (1988) 'Teachers and principals: Turf, tension, and new tasks', *Phi Delta Kappan* **69**, pp. 648–53.
PORTER, A.C. (1987) 'Teacher collaboration: New partnerships to attack old problems', *Phi Delta Kappan* **69**, pp. 147–52.
SARASON, S.B. (1971) *The Culture of School and the Problem of Change*, Boston, Allyn and Bacon, Inc.

Section Three: The Effective Principal and the Curriculum
Caryl B. Burns
Granite Falls Middle School, North Carolina

Every evening Caryl Burns telephones five parents — sometimes about a particular issue, but often just to say 'hello' and see if they have anything they would like to discuss. Every month she writes a newsletter that is mailed to parents and community leaders, keeping them informed of the latest news. But improving communications is only one of her many goals. When she became principal of Granite Falls Middle School, Burns noticed that faculty and staff rarely attended workshops or seminars, so she brought staff development programs to the school. After analyzing the curriculum, she decided to extend the school day by one period in order to add foreign language, art, advanced math, occupation exploration and chorus. As a result, test scores improved, especially in writing, where her students exceed state and local averages. Burns received her BA from Lenoir-Rhyne College, an MA from Appalachian State University, and an EdD from the University of North Carolina.

The principalship has changed and the traditional view of the principal as the instructional leader of the school is often dismissed as an ideal that can never be achieved in America's schools. Research into the daily activities of the school principal indicates a move toward a role as a professional manager for the nation's school leaders. From the nineteenth century role as the school's 'head teacher', to the twentieth century role as a school manager and instructional supervisor, to the emerging role as the professional manager, the principal's daily work is characterized by 'fragmentation, brevity, verbal (as opposed to written) communication, physical movement, one-to-one interactions, interruptions, and crisis' (McCurdy, 1983, p. 12).

How do principals feel concerning their role in instruction? Research done by Blumberg and Greenfield indicates that principals consider personnel and program development as their most important tasks (Blumberg and Greenfield, 1980, p. 4). Blumberg further states,

> While many principals might dream of being effective instructional leaders by enhancing the activities of teaching and learning in their schools, in reality their experience is shaped by the press of administrative and managerial functions that mitigate against that dream becoming fact. (*ibid*, p. 6)

Research by Van Cleve Morris and his associates reported in the *AASA Critical Issues Report* indicates principals have the training and the knowledge to plan, develop, advise, direct, and evaluate instruction. They appear to be generally well read and generally aware of recent trends in teaching practices (Weldy, 1989, p. 2). Putting what principals know into practice is a critical issue facing education. The number of recent reports challenging the credibility of American education indicate Americans intend for instruction to be the prime focus of the schools. Principals really have no choice. In this period of declining student achievement, wavering public confidence in schools, and demands for financial accountability, principals must furnish instructional leadership whether they want to or not. 'If they don't have time, they must find time. If they don't know how, they must learn' (Weldy, 1989, p. 3).

Selection of content for the curriculum is a problem that will probably never be settled. The debate is especially intensified with any national crisis. The launching of Sputnik in 1957 is a good example of the crises that impacted our educational system.

Three recent books have been most critical of our schools' curriculum. In *Cultural Literacy: What Every American Needs to Know*, E.D. Hirsch Jr. contends that many students, especially those from deprived homes, do not read well because they do not have the background knowledge to understand what they are supposed to read. This network of information, he contends, allows a person to read a newspaper and read it with an adequate level of comprehension, getting the point, grasping the implications, relating what they read to unstated context, which alone gives meaning to what they read (Hirsch, 1988, p. 2). Hirsch then lists 5000 essential names, phrases, dates, and concepts that he believes every American needs to know.

Allan Bloom in *The Closing of the American Mind* details the shortcomings of higher education and the public schools. He feels students are not ready for college and they lack the basic knowledge students had twenty to twenty-five years ago (Bloom, 1987, p. 30). A good example of Bloom's proposal applies in the state of North Carolina where 464 remedial courses were taught in 1989 within the college system — twenty six per institution.

In *What Do Our 17-Year-Olds Know?*, Diane Ravitch and Chester Finn Jr. report that students cannot tell the half century in which the Civil War occurred or who wrote *Leaves of Grass*. They call for more time to be spent in history and literature at all levels (Ravitch and Finn, 1987, p. 21).

On Becoming the Instructional Leader

How does the principal become the instructional leader of the school? The principal is in a strategic position to provide the essential elements for curriculum development, implementation and evaluation. Some of the key areas in which a principal can become an effective leader include:

Personnel The principal should employ the best teachers possible. He should provide an inservice program for new and experienced teachers with the aim of constantly improving the instructional program.

Instructional Support The principal should provide support by reducing class disruptions and by involving teachers, students and parents in the resolution of school problems such as absenteeism.

Adequate Resources The principal maintains quality control of the instructional program and of student progress. He monitors all data to determine the need for increased support.

Coordination of Activities The principal coordinates the many activities of the school to see that the total curriculum is aligned. An important area for coordination is the time for instructional personnel to plan together and to share information concerning the progress of the students.

Problem Solving Effective principals know what is going on through regular meetings, daily tours of the school, and conversations with the students and staff. (McCurdy, 1983, pp. 20–1)

The most important characteristic for a principal in being an instructional leader is to make everyone at the school aware of the importance of curriculum as it relates to the total school program; the very heartbeat of the school. Successful principals insist that every teacher be well prepared every day with interesting, challenging lessons and activities. The principal can often be seen in classrooms observing, offering support and suggestions. Challenging inservice is offered for the teachers and the emphasis on the instructional mission of the schools gives a sense of purpose to what happens in the school on a daily basis.

The effective principal is sensitive to the history and culture of the school setting. He is aware of factors that influence the curriculum. Some of these factors include the local community, pressure groups, accrediting agencies, textbooks, state departments of public instruction, local school district offices and testing agencies.

The principal who is committed to instruction uses the curriculum to present a clear vision for the school. He is able to define the vision through slogans, themes, logos and reminders. He provides enthusiasm and support for the total school program and never lets the staff forget the mission of the school (Smith and Andrews, 1985, p. 37).

What Shall We Teach or What is Worth Knowing?

Based on the philosophy of the school, a crucial element in the total instructional program is the selection of what will be taught. It is obvious that everything available and teachable in the culture cannot be included in the curriculum. The knowledge explosion doubles and triples every few years and educators are often frustrated with the magnitude of the material they are expected to teach in a short school year. The last decade has brought new programs and emphasis to the curriculum including drug, sex and multicultural education, thinking skills, education for global understanding, technological education with emphasis on computers, education for economic understanding, arts education and training to become a lifelong learner.

Educators must take all the 'givens' and the length of time available, which may be 180 days, more or less, and make tough decisions concerning what will be taught and taught well during instruction time. Many of the content decisions will have already been made by county and state curriculum mandates. Schools must consider the curriculum, however, especially in the areas of minimum versus enriched curricula, competencies and preferences of the faculty, the academic status of the students, and for accountability in testing programs.

A State Plan for Curriculum

In 1984, the North Carolina State Department of Public Instruction began a revision of the *North Carolina Standard Course of Study* and the initial development of the *North Carolina Competency-Based Curriculum*. Three publications focused on efforts that involved thousands of educators across the state. *The Basic Education Program for North Carolina's Public Schools* outlines the curricula, general standards, materials support and staffing which should be provided in all schools throughout the state. *The North Carolina Standard Course of Study*, adopted by the State Board of Education, provides an overview of the basic curriculum which should be made available to every child in the public schools of the state. *The North Carolina Competency-Based Curriculum,* known as the Teacher Handbook by educators, provides recommended goals, objectives, and suggested measures for each subject or skill area. Areas included in the statewide curriculum are arts education, communication skills, guidance, healthful living, library and media skills, mathematics, science, second language and social studies, and vocational education.

The Teacher Handbook for the curriculum is quite specific. One area, for instance, the communication skills curriculum, is as follows:

Grade Level: 8
Skills/Subject Area: Reading/Literature
COMPETENCY GOAL 7: The learner will identify story elements in various types of literature to aid in comprehension.

Objectives	*Measures*
7.4 Determine the mood of a selection.	7.4.1 Underline phrases in a passage which determine mood.
	7.4.2 Select the word or phrase which shows the mood of an historical novel
	7.4.3 List all words or phrases which are associated with the mood of a given story.

| 7.5 Determine the theme of a selection. | 7.5.1 Make a collage of photographs that depict the theme of a story. |
| | 7.5.2 Compare several stories and make a list of those with similar themes. |

(North Carolina Department of Public Instruction, 1985, p. 236)

What is the role of the principal and the local school when the curriculum is detailed from the state level? The task of determining what will be taught becomes somewhat easier in state-mandated curricula, but educators are well aware that the statewide program of studies is a minimum program. Schools are expected to go far beyond the minimum standards. The main responsibilities of the principal in a curriculum that is designed on a statewide basis is to be knowledgeable of the entire program and to determine and ensure that teachers are following the program in their classroom instruction.

One area for curriculum development which is effective in all types of arrangements is integrated learning experiences. Integrated learning refers to the interrelatedness of subject and skill areas within and across grade levels. Integrated learning is one of the simplest, but often most neglected techniques to tie various subject and skill areas together.

Leaders in education have called for integrated programs for years. Over three decades age, Ralph Tyler designated curricular integration as one of three criteria needed to build an effective organization of learning experiences. He defined integration as 'the horizontal relationship of curriculum experiences' and viewed it as a 'must' to help students gain a unified view of their learning (Tyler, 1949, p. 181).

Thirty five years later, Goodlad, in *A Place Called School*, reported that a major problem in schooling was the 'degree of unconnectedness it often has with the reality beyond school'. Goodlad also pointed to the fragmentation between and among programs and recommended a close articulation of elementary, middle and senior high schools (Goodlad, 1984, p. 38).

Ernest Boyer, a former Commissioner of Education, criticized schools for presenting segmented, isolated subjects. He called for a curriculum that would help students understand a complex, integrated world. He maintained that students needed a program that allowed them to see relationships that add up to life (Boyer, 1983, p. 137).

Many teachers have routinely integrated learning areas for students. It is the principal, however, who is in a position to help present learning in a holistic, meaningful way. Principals themselves can be knowledgeable about appropriate possibilities for integration. Principals also play a central role in determining the overall school organization as well as the day-to-day schedule. Providing common planning periods, limiting pull-out programs, initiating disciplinary and interdisciplinary grade level teams and committees and protecting instructional time are ways a principal can help bring about integration of learning. Principals can also provide assistance with facilities when teachers need to use halls, cafeterias, auditoriums and other areas necessary for additional work space. In all phases of integrated learning, the principal plays a key role in providing the time, resources and facilities to assist teachers in their work.

Evaluating the Instructional Program

Part of the job of an instructional leader is to evaluate the instructional program and the teachers. How can a principal approach this important task? Characteristics of an excellent evaluation program include the following:

the goals, objectives and purposes of the school are clearly stated and have been communicated to all teachers, staff, students and the community;

the procedures to be used in formal evaluations are based on research and on common understandings of what is good teaching and what makes a good school;

teachers know and understand the criteria by which they are to be evaluated;

evaluations are as valid and as reliable as possible;

evaluations are more diagnostic than judgmental;

self-evaluation is an important objective of the program;

the self-image and self-respect of teachers are maintained and enhanced;

the evaluation process encourages teachers to be creative and to experiment with the learning experiences provided for children;

the evaluation process makes ample provision for clear, personalized and constructive feedback;

teacher evaluation is seen as an important part of the instructional role of the principal and of the inservice program for teachers. (American Association of School Administrators, 1982, p. 10)

Supervising and evaluating the teaching process are two of the main responsibilities of the effective principal. Through regular observation, the principal is able to know the strengths, weaknesses, styles and personalities of the teaching staff. By observing teachers, the principal has the responsibility 'to compliment the accomplished, support the inexperienced, counsel with the specialists and correct or eliminate the incompetent' (Schon, 1983, p. 20).

Evaluating becomes difficult when principals do not feel confident of their own knowledge of instruction. Since most of them have been teachers prior to becoming principals, they know the feelings teachers have about principals who visit when in their classrooms once or twice during the year and then make judgments concerning their competence as a teacher. The most difficult part of the entire process is to conference with the teacher, especially if it is a veteran teacher, and tell them they need to improve.

Even for principals who do manage to make frequent visits to the classrooms, the task of making a record of all of the data can become laborious. Most evaluation instruments are designed with the idea in mind that if you did not write the information down while observing a class, it did not happen. The principal is then faced with the problem of being able to adequately assess his observations and write it down at the same time. Time then becomes a crucial factor in effectively evaluating teachers and the total school program.

How Do I Find Time to Be the Instructional Leader?

Most principals rank time as the number one factor that prevents them from being the instructional leader they would like to be. The principal is expected to be all things to all people and the demands on his time and energy become so exhausting that they drain the enthusiasm and creativity that could make good principals excellent ones. Time management and its relationship with information management are crucial factors in improving the effectiveness of school leaders.

One step in time management is improvement of goal setting and prioritizing. While most principals have a set of goals and are adept in prioritizing, they constantly let others rearrange the priorities for them. The successful instructional leader makes instruction a top priority throughout the school. The priority is communicated to everyone including the faculty, staff and students.

A second step in time management is to periodically keep a time log. Management consultants recommend that administrators keep some type of written daily log for at least a week to track their use of time. An analysis of the log will reveal if time is being filled with time-wasters.

A third step in time management is to control the time-wasters. These wasters may include visitors, telephone calls, meetings, paperwork, procrastination, the inability to say 'no', scheduling ineffectively and delegating inappropriately.

Finally, to be the instructional leader that he would like to be, the principal must develop a system within the school to gather comprehensive information concerning what is going on. The principal must have ready and accurate information on a wide range of things including attendance, discipline, grades, maintenance, budget, teacher observation data, and much more. Using technology and other methods and procedures, the principal who wants to be the effective instructional leader must have fast and accurate access to information that can be used in problem solving, decision making, implementation and monitoring of programs.

With sufficient information and training, the principal is able to reflect in action, on action and while in action. He is able to reflect about problems rather than acting impulsively, using his base of knowledge and infomation; he is able to reflect on action that has already occurred and determine if changes need to be made within the school and its program; he is able to reflect while in action, which suggests that he is able to be on 'automatic pilot', with professional outlines while engaging in critical inquiry about other things (Schon, 1983, p. 20).

Case Study

Principal Paul became the principal at Mountain Top School following the retirement of Principal Sam. The school, located in a small middle class community, enjoys wide community support. The central office has been generally pleased with the school and the progress made at the school over the years.

The faculty is composed mostly of teachers with fifteen or more years of experience. Because of the relative stability of the faculty, few new teachers have been hired for the last eight years. Improvements at the school have been largely physical or technological, with extensive landscaping projects and a new media wing constructed. In addition, computers have been added to nearly every classroom, as well as extensive video equipment. The consensus is that the school is attractive and up-to-date.

During the first few weeks at the school, Principal Paul studied test data for the school since the school is involved in the statewide testing program. Several disturbing facts emerged. The scores for Mountain Top School appeared 'flat', ranking at or just below the system-wide averages for the last five years. A closer analysis revealed that the students who did not achieve near their potential were those students who were average or slightly above average in their academic aptitude.

Before confronting the teachers, Principal Paul observed his teachers over the course of the next several weeks. He visited classrooms, asked about teaching strategies and observed the students. All of the teachers kept lesson plans and appeared to be enthusiastic about what they were teaching. Principal Paul noticed that almost all of the teachers had old state adopted textbooks in their classrooms. He noticed that these books were often used and were, in some cases, issued to the students in lieu of the current adoption. In the book storage center, many current text adoption titles were shelved, along with accompanying workbooks and materials for those texts.

Further investigation revealed a high percentage of instructional monies at the school being spent on supplementary texts, workbooks and duplicating masters. The amount of paper used over the last few years had tripled and the school had consistently overrun its allotment for xerox copies. Teachers appeared to be copying and duplicating more materials for classroom use.

Principal Paul had several meetings with the grade level representatives to discuss test scores and instructional materials in the school. The teachers seemed interested in performing well on statewide testing, but could offer no explanation for past performance. When asked about the use of old textbooks, the teachers noted that the new ones were not as good as the old ones. In many subject areas the new books were attractive and well illustrated, but were simply too easy for students and provided too few guided practice opportunities for the students. These texts were viewed as too elementary for the school needs.

Several weeks later, Principal Paul mentioned to one of the teachers that a televised special would be on the next evening dealing with one of the countries studied in the sixth grade social studies curriculum. A suggestion was made to tape the program for the students to see the next week. The teacher mentioned that he did not teach that particular unit in social studies, although it was required.

Over the next month, Principal Paul concluded that the teachers did not follow the statewide curriculum. An examination of the copies of the various subject area components housed in the media center were infrequently checked out, and like the state adopted texts, were only used for shelving. Nonetheless, the teachers worked hard, taught their lessons well, and generally were satisfied, as was the community, with their program of instruction.

Before the end of the semester, Principal Paul met with the curriculum supervisor to discuss the problems he had observed at Mountain Top School. Considering the faculty, the academic aptitude of the students, the test scores, and state mandates for performance, how can Principal Paul align the program of instruction with the state adopted program, while at the same time enlist the support and cooperation of the staff?

Key Points

1 The principalship has changed from the concept of 'head teacher' to the instructional supervisor, to the professional manager.
2 In this period of declining student achievement and wavering public confidence, principals must furnish instructional leadership.
3 The instructional leader must have an understanding of the factors affecting curriculum, a clear concept of what should be taught, knowledge of curriculum construction and implementation, along with an understanding of effective evaluative techniques.
4 Time management and its relationship to information management are crucial factors in improving the work of school leaders.
5 To be the instructional leader, the principal must develop a system within the school to gather information so that effective decisions can be made.

Discussion Questions

1 How can the principal respond to state-mandated curriculum initiatives while providing for individual teacher input in curriculum design?
2 How do you begin curriculum development that reflects horizontal and vertical articulation?
3 How can needs assessment instruments be effectively utilized in curriculum development?
4 What are some effects of the school reform movement that will impact curriculum for under-represented children?
5 What information sources does Burns identify in developing the curriculum?

References

AMERICAN ASSOCIATION OF SCHOOL ADMINISTRATORS (1982) *Evaluating Educational Personnel*, Arlington, VA.

BLOOM, A. (1987) *The Closing of the American Mind*, New York, Simon & Schuster.

BLUMBERG, A. and GREENFIELD, W. (1980) *The Effective Principal*, Boston, Allyn & Bacon.

BOYER, E.L. (1983) *High School: A Report on Secondary Education in America*, New York, Harper & Row.

GOODLAD, J.I. (1984) *A Place Called School*, New York, McGraw-Hill.

HIRSCH, E.D., JR. (1988) *Cultural Literacy: What Every American Needs to Know*, New York, Random House.

McCurdy, J. (1983) *The Role of the Principal in Effective Schools: Problems and Solutions*, Sacramento, American Association of School Administrators.

North Carolina Department of Public Instruction (1985) *North Carolina Competency-Based Curriculum: The Teacher Handbook*, Raleigh.

Ravitch, D. and Finn, C.E., Jr. (1987) *What Do Our 17-Year-Olds Know? A Report of the First National Assessment of History and Literature*, New York, Harper & Row.

Schon, D.A. (1983) *The Reflective Practitioner: How Principals Think in Action*, New York, Basic Books.

Smith, W.F. and Andrews, R.L. (1985) 'Clinical supervision for principals', *Educational Leadership*, **45**, pp. 34–7.

Tyler, R. (1949) *Basic Principles of Curriculum and Instruction*, Chicago, University of Chicago Press.

Weldy, G.R. (1989) *Principals: What They Do and Who They Are*, NASSP Monograph.

Section Four: Organizational Factors
Susan L. Van Zant
Pomerado Elementary School, California

After twenty-one years as an educator, Susan Van Zant knows how to respond to the needs of her students, parents, teachers, and community. In 1981, when she was assigned to Garden Road Elementary School, a school with the lowest academic scores in the district, Van Zant first raised achievement expectations for all students and then mobilized teachers and parents to work together to meet their needs. With their input and backing, she applied for grants and implemented programs on drug resistance, hands-on science instruction, school-age child care, crime prevention and nutrition education. By 1987, when she moved to her present position, Garden Road had earned the California Distinguished School Award. Van Zant received a BA from Long Beach State University, an MA from Northern Arizona University, and an EdD from the United States International University in San Diego.

Demographics

Changes in demographics have a profound effect upon education. Within California there is a rapidly growing minority population and an aging Anglo population. By the year 2000, it is anticipated that 48 per cent of California's population will be Hispanic, Asian or African American. Ninety-two per cent of the people in California will live in a county with at least 30 per cent Hispanic, Asian or African American population. Within the Poway Unified School District, administrators keep current on population changes in their schools' attendance area. In this way they are prepared to meet challenges as they occur.

The Poway Unified School District with twenty one schools and 23,000 students is located approximately twenty miles north of downtown San Diego and twenty miles from the coast. It encompasses more than a hundred square miles. The boundaries of the District include the City of Poway as well as a northern portion of the City of San Diego. Principals within this system realize the importance of good community relations. A well organized two-way communication system provides a window to the school. It encourages not only parent, but community involvement in the educational program for all students.

Over the past five years population trends within San Diego County, and more specifically within the Poway Unified School District, have changed. Every year there is a larger proportion of minority students. Many of these children do not speak English. There is a wide diversity of languages spoken at home. The largest minority population within the District is Filipino. This growth brings with it not only a need to provide additional facilities, but also a responsibility to meet the needs of an ethnically diverse student population. The District, sensitive to concerns regarding fair and equitable treatment of Filipino students, began action to address the issues. The District focused on actively recruiting additional Filipino staff, installed a Community Awareness telephone contact at a local high school and established a broad-based Ethnic Relations Investigation implemented to help bridge language and/or cultural differences.

In the past twenty years there has been a dramatic change in the number of mothers of school age children who are now part of the work force. It is now unusual for a mother of a school age child to stay home. A 1989 review of Pomerado Elementary School records indicated that only four per cent of the mothers did not either have a job outside the home or provide child care for women who did.

This change was recognized by the principals and adjustments in the home-school program have been undertaken. Scheduling parent conferences at times convenient to parent work schedules, conducting programs for parents in the evening, and establishing a student day care program at the school site are some ways schools have reorganized to meet changing needs within the community.

Organizing a school which has the support of the staff and community is a major challenge facing principals today. Sound and constructive relationships must be developed and maintained so that the school can function effectively by providing all students with the essential skills and knowledge needed to become contributing members of society. The need for communication has grown rapidly in recent years. This growth has been stimulated to a considerable extent by the cultural and technological changes taking place in society and by the emergence of new and critical problems confronting schools today. There is a desire on the part of the public and teachers to increase their involvement in affairs of the school. The development and use of a strong communication network is one strategy that principals should not overlook.

Communication Sources

A communication network should be designed to promote a better understanding of the school, interpret public attitudes, and foster involvement in school affairs. The development of a comprehensive program requires the following three steps: an accurate assessment of the status of current cooperative efforts; the creation of a vision of how two-way communication can work effectively for the betterment of the school; and the development of a plan of action to close the gap between the vision and the current status.

The principal should identify a communication network team. Members of the key communicators' team should include parents, teachers and interested members of the community. These people need to meet together in order to gather and review data. They also need to create a vision which demonstrates the school's commitment to building a sound communication network. It should serve as a guide for staff, parents and community as they work together.

The team then needs to develop a plan of action. The plan should identify both long and short term goals at both the classroom and school-wide levels. For example, a short term class goal may be to send home a weekly class newsletter. A long term school goal might be to implement a motivational home reading program.

As in any good planning program, the principal should take care to ensure that implementation is monitored. Progress towards goals should be checked regularly and modifications made as needed. Activities need to be evaluated to see if they move the school closer to the vision.

To ensure effective communication it is necessary to obtain factual knowledge and an understanding of the people who make up the community. The more that is known about them, the better the chances are of designing a program that will be successful. Population characteristics concerning age, single parent families, occupation, race, creed and nationality are useful information sources. These data can be obtained through school records or from the US Census report.

Surveying parents is a way to gather information about their concerns, as well as to communicate to parents the concerns of the school. Parent opinion can be solicited through written surveys that are sent home or included in the school newsletter. Telephone interviews are a way to ensure that more parents will be represented in a survey. Parent surveys should be conducted periodically and the results reported in the local press, shared in the school newsletter and discussed with the faculty. Survey results can be used to gain insights into school problems and to implement an effective communication program.

In the Poway Unified School District, a parent attitude survey is conducted every other spring. A random sample of households are surveyed. In an endeavor to obtain responses from at least 90 per cent of the random sample, each household in the sample is telephoned. An independent research service is contracted to conduct the survey to assure anonymity of specific responders. In the spring of 1989, 2035 responses were obtained from a total of 2246 sampled households.

This opinion research is indispensable is planning, conducting and evaluating the school-community relations program. It is used to determine how people get information about the schools, how parents judge the quality of their children's education, what their general satisfaction or dissatisfaction is with the individual schools and with the School District, what problems must be identified and solved, and what their views on projected changes are within the district, such as possible year round school scheduling or a district name change.

As an extra dividend, opinion research actually stimulates the individuals who are contacted to form opinions about the subjects being investigated. Individuals who have not thought seriously about the school programs are forced to do some thinking about them when their opinions are being sought in such a research study. Moreover, by communicating with the schools, they believe they have given valuable and important responses.

Parent Involvement

A strong school communication network emphasizes parent involvement. Research shows and educators have always known that children do better in school if their parents are involved in their education. Everyone profits when parents read to their children, encourage them to do well and support the school. What principals have not always realized is that they can greatly increase the amount and type of parent involvement. Parents who have been successful in school often automatically play an active role in their children's learning and success in school. Many other parents want to help, but they are sometimes unsure as to what they can or should do to support their children. Principals cannot afford to leave parent involvement to chance. They must make a conscious, carefully planned, and continuous effort to include all parents in their children's education.

Research indicates when the school involves parents in home learning activities, parents develop positive attitudes toward the school.

Epstein (1986) found that when teachers involved parents in home learning activities the parents reported that:

they believed that they should help their children at home;

they had a larger collection of ideas to use at home;

they increased understanding of school programs;

they rated the teacher higher in overall teaching quality;

they recognized teacher efforts and rated them higher than other teachers on interpersonal skills.

School wide programs which involve parents also impact student learning. Gordon (1978) indicated that programs designed with strong parent involvement produced students who perform better than those in otherwise identical programs that do not involve parents as thoroughly or that do not involve them at all.

All types of parent involvement and efforts to establish two-way communication initiated by the school can have impact. However, a successful home involvement program requires organizational support from the principal. To ensure its acceptance, parent involvement must be viewed as a legitimate activity of the school. Rich (1986) noted, 'Reaching the family must be considered as important as reaching the child.' Programs must be well planned, comprehensive and long-lasting. Programs which reinforce interaction between teacher and parents are likely to have the greatest impact on student achievement (Gordon, 1978).

Reporting to Parents

Within the Poway Unified School District, parent conferences are scheduled for a week in November. During this time, students attend school on a minimum-day schedule. Conferences are held so that parents and teachers can express themselves more completely and openly. Misunderstandings and misconceptions can also be more quickly clarified in face-to-face meetings by asking questions and elaborating on specific points.

With so many parents working it is important to conduct conferences at times that are convenient for them. Early morning and late appointments are popular. In scheduling conferences adequate time to discuss the child's progress must be allowed.

Creating a positive and welcoming environment contributes to an effective conference. It is important for the principal to remind teachers of the power they have in a conference. Teachers set the tone of a conference by how they establish rapport and organize the conference. This meeting should be more than a verbal report card, for example, sharing of test results with parents. To be most useful, the conference needs to convey how much progress the child had made since the beginning of the school year. Teachers need to listen and be understanding. The teacher and the parent then need to plan how they will work together to help the child have success during the remainder of the school year. An effective parent conference should accomplish several goals:

teachers gain information about the child's home environment;

parents and teachers gain a greater appreciation for the child's unique talents and interests;

parents obtain information about their child's academic progress and expectations for this school year;

parents get answers to questions about school policies and practices;

the teacher and parent determine how they will work together to enable the child to experience success in school.

Throughout the year, report cards provide important information to students and parents. However, the effectiveness is limited by the infrequency of the reporting periods. Interim progress reports are informal teacher-made weekly progress notes to parents and an effective means of communicating with families. These reports provide information before official report cards are issued and allow parents to work with their child to improve or maintain progress.

Messages to Parents

Letters and personal messages from principals and the instructional staff can lead to positive relationships between home and school. Principals should encourage teachers to send introductory letters to parents on or before the first day of school. These letters give parents background information about the teacher, positive expectations about the upcoming school year, and present an image of a person who is genuinely interested in the students. These letters make it easier for parents to interact with teachers, and provide a vehicle for preparing parents to expect more communication throughout the year. The format, color or distinguishing logo that will be used on notes and newsletters all year can be used and explained. This is also the ideal time to begin two-way communication. Letters can include a tear-off portion to be returned to the teacher completed by the parent indicating when they are available for telephone contact, conferences or to help in the classroom. Teachers may also want to ask parents to answer a few questions about their child.

Throughout the year teachers should be encouraged to send home notes and make telephone calls commenting on things students do well. These notes may describe outstanding classwork, improvements in study habits, acts of courtesy, special talents, and other positive behaviors. Parents who receive these notes and phone calls feel pleased and grateful for the information. Positive communication can balance the negative impact should a child happen to experience difficulty later in the year. An established positive rapport can serve to help deal with a problem. Some teachers like to keep continuous record of who they call and what was discussed. In the same manner, principals should take time to write letters of commendation to parents when students make a contribution to the school such as volunteering for the safety patrol, assisting in the library, or serving as student body officer. Positive messages reinforce student academic performance and behavior. They also help support other ongoing home-school communication activities.

Principals should also encourage teachers to send home classroom newsletters. They are an excellent way to keep in touch with parents and help them be a part of their child's education. Frequent and regular class newsletters enable parents to sense the feeling and momentum of the class. They are a good way to let parents know what is being studied in different curricular areas, remind them about upcoming events and present parent education information. If English is not the language spoken at home, newsletters should be translated, if possible.

Thank you letters can be sent to homes of students at the end of the school year. This gives the teacher the opportunity to express appreciation for parent and student contributions to the class. They may also offer ideas which parents can use to reinforce skills learned during the school year, recommend interesting summer activities, and resources which may be useful during the vacation period.

School Handbooks/Newsletters

Schools use handbooks or printed portfolios as a means to communicate general information about the school to parents, students, and school personnel. Useful handbooks reflect the school's philosophy, mission statement, purpose, as well as daily schedules, a school map, listings of holidays, homework policy and other general information.

School newsletters are an effective means of communicating with parents and the community in general. The newsletter must be frequent (at least once a month) and consistent since it is setting the precedent for home-school communication. Well organized principals find it helpful to create a file of useful articles and topics which may be included in future issues. By including mini-surveys for parent response on critical topics the newsletters may be a valuable two-way communication and information gathering tool. The format should be attractive and easy to read. Copies should be sent to District office personnel, key members of the community and the local press.

Meetings

Meetings are a valuable tool for communicating and involving parents in the educational process. Meetings provide face-to-face contact that is essential in building the rapport, trust, and understanding necessary for parents and the school to work as partners. An important goal for all meetings is to convey information about the school and its programs, as well as to initiate and maintain a positive feeling about the school. The following meeting ideas are some that have worked successfully. They include beginning-of-the-year meetings, special meetings that encourage ongoing home-school communication, and meetings that involve parents and students in learning activities.

Parent orientation evenings

Within the first few weeks of school the principal should schedule a series of evening parent meetings. Each grade should have a separate time to meet with parents. This allows parents with more than one child in the school to attend all necessary meetings. During the orientation, teachers explain the curriculum for the year, the essential skills and knowledge which will be taught, standards of expected behavior, homework policies, as well as respond to parent questions. In addition, it is a wonderful opportunity for teachers to explain to parents how they can become active participants in their child's education.

Open house

Parents are most likely to attend and be positively influenced by an Open House if their own child's work is featured in some way, or there are presentations involving many children. It has proven to be effective to feature school-wide Literary Arts Fairs where student writing and art work is placed on display. A Science Fair is also a high interest event. To be most successful these endeavors require much preparation, advance planning and publicity from the principal's office. Parent volunteers can also play an active role in organizing these special events.

Neighborhood gatherings

Small groups of ten to twelve parents are invited to meet informally with the principal in a community member's home to discuss issues. These informal meetings are an excellent way to explain new textbook adoptions, a teaching strategy such as cooperative learning, and/or to answer questions. These gatherings are often a way to become acquainted with reluctant parents who usually shy away from school activities. Principals must make an effort to become involved in community activities. Local community events such as Kiwanis breakfasts, ten-K runs, and picnics are not only interesting to attend, but help the principal gain valuable insights about the community.

Grandparents day
One way to build communication that has been successful at the local middle school is to invite senior citizens and grandparents to attend school for a day as a special guest. Often grandparents are the family members with open time during school hours. Their better understanding of the school program, expectations and positive impressions of the school are communicated to parents and other members of the community. Activities can include opportunities for seniors and children to discuss 'how things and times have changed'.

Family enrichment events
Families and the staff gather together for an evening or special day in which they share a variety of learning activities. Family Math is a home-learning program developed by the University California Equals Project, and has proven to be effective in increasing student achievement, and building positive attitudes toward math. Volunteer staff members and parents are trained to be facilitators for a series of weekly evening sessions where families come together to learn to play math games, solve problems, and enjoy being together. Most series last about a month. Teachers organize, teach and participate in the different activities.

As a spin off from Family Math, a mentor teacher within the Poway school system developed a series of Science Night Seminars. This program is extremely popular and is offered throughout the year in order to meet the demand.

Study and discussion groups
Study and discussion groups have grown rapidly ever since parents have indicated a desire to become more involved in the schools. Such groups represent an increasing concern and a desire on the part of the parents to know more about the schools their children attend. These groups fall into two main classes. One such class is concerned with the policies and practices of the school, and methods by which parents and teacher can work together. Discussions center around such subjects as homework, discipline, health, social hygiene education, drug and substance abuse prevention. Also, the teaching strategies are covered in detail for parents who wish to know how to help their children at home.

Parenting study seminars are another broad category that has attracted wide attention. Guided by a competent professional, parents learn how to interpret behavior patterns of children and what to expect from their children as they progress from one developmental stage to another. Parents are also directed to additional reading materials, and assisted in analyzing motives that lie behind inappropriate behavior. They also learn how to develop and keep lines of communication open with their children as they grow older. Through parenting classes, they come to understand their own children better.

Student recognition programs

Student recognition programs are another way to promote communication with parents. Monthly Good Citizens assemblies provide the format that highlights student achievement. Not only can two students from each classroom be identified as the good citizens of the month, but other students can be recognized for achievement in specific areas. Awards can be presented to spelling bee winners, members of the 100 per cent club, student authors, as well as for participation in physical education, service activities, and student council events.

These programs promote a sense of pride in the school and encourage students to do their best in school. Since these assemblies are usually held during school hours, invitations should be sent to parents well in advance of the program. Often times when parents cannot attend, friends and relatives are willing to attend in their place.

Homework

Homework is a regular routine for most students. Walberg, Paschal and Weinstein (1985) found that well designed and appropriate homework can significantly increase learning time, and if homework is graded or commented upon by the teacher, it results in increased student achievement on tests. Homework is also a valuable communication tool. Most teachers assign homework to give students time to practice skills they have learned in class. It provides a window on the classroom for parents. They can see the kinds of skills their children are learning and gain insights into successes and difficulties their children are having with school. It is our sincere intent to further increase the cooperation between the home and school in order to provide the best possible learning process for the students of Pomerado. By working with teachers to adopt a school-wide homework policy, the principal can build a positive homework climate which supports teacher efforts. The school can help parents become involved in their child's education by effectively communicating information to parents about the homework policy and procedures. Homework policies can be distributed to parents through handbooks, parent orientation evening, and messages sent by each teacher. The information provided to parents should answer the following questions:

Why are students assigned homework?

How often is homework assigned?

How will homework be graded?

How will homework grades be reported and used?

How much homework will be assigned (minutes/hours per day) in each grade level?

What are parent responsibilities in regard to homework?

How can parents help with homework?

Homework policy
To recognize the importance of providing additional learning opportunities for students and foster students' sense of responsibility toward academic achievement, the teachers of Pomerado assign homework to students. Specific grade level homework procedures are developed at the beginning of each school year.

Students are given homework assignments based upon individual needs. The purpose of the homework is to reinforce skills which have been previously taught in school and/or enrich the learning experience. Students who are absent from school for any reason should complete class assignments.

Parents should provide a quiet, well-lighted location for their children to work on their homework. Children should have a specific time set aside each day to complete their homework. When a child has completed an assignment, it is important that an adult check over the work to make sure it is complete and neat before it is returned to school.

Telephone Answering Machines

Schools can efficiently use automatic telephone answering machines to provide information to parents on a call-in basis. They can relate information on topics similar to those addressed in school newsletters, but in an oral rather than written form. Messages can be recorded in the languages spoken by the parents.

The telephone answering machine is especially useful for parent notification of student absences or tardies. This device permits parents to contact the school at times convenient to them, when the office may not be open. Within the Poway school system clerical staff calls parents to notify them promptly when a student is absent or tardy. School personnel makes sure that parents know that they should notify the school promptly whenever a student is absent or late, and that it is their responsibility to see that the child gets to school regularly, and on time.

Volunteers

Schools that use volunteers in their programs also exhibit a strong home-school communication program. A volunteer coordinator is one of the keys to building a successful volunteer program. This person provides the needed connection between the parent community and the school which enables a volunteer program to work smoothly and effectively. The volunteer coordinator has several important roles and responsibilities:

identify the need for volunteers and potential jobs;

recruit and place volunteers;

train and provide on-going support for volunteers;

maintain records and document volunteer contributions;

recognize and reward volunteers;

evaluate the volunteer program.

The effectiveness of a volunteer program can be strengthened by training both volunteers and teachers. Volunteers need to have an orientation which explains their role and the general expectations regarding working with students at the school.

Comprehensive workshops and training sessions can be offered to all volunteers on such topics as curriculum materials for assisting with reading, math, science, social studies. Special sessions should be designed for volunteers working in the school library office, or in the teachers' work-room.

The principal can support volunteers by communicating with them. Each volunteer should receive a handbook which describes general school procedures, daily schedules, a map of the school, useful volunteer tips, as well as an outline of volunteers' responsibilities. The principal should set aside a room in which the volunteer coordinator and the volunteers can work and spend their break time. At one school a custodian storeroom was cleaned out and painted by the principal and proved to be a good space for volunteers. Time for interaction with the coordinator and the principal is helpful to both the volunteer and the teacher. Volunteers can get questions answered and raise issues that are of importance to them. If separate space is not available, some place should be located where volunteers, the coordinator and the principal can meet regularly.

Training for teachers should center on ways to effectively use and communicate with volunteers. Teachers may need help in learning the management skills required to work effectively with volunteers.

It is important for the coordinator to provide parents, staff and the school with a periodic report of volunteer activities. Such a report helps all to see how much is being contributed and builds momentum for the program.

Most people volunteer because they want to help and feel useful. However, even adults need feedback and encouragement to know how they are doing. Schools need to support volunteers through recognition of their contributions and through expressions of gratitude for the significant part they play in meeting student needs. The principal needs to highlight parent volunteers in newsletters, news articles in the local press and at school meetings. The recognition of volunteers needs to be ongoing, not just at the end of the year, teas and luncheons. Some schools furnish name tags for volunteers to wear each time they are working on campus. This enables all school staff to recognize, welcome, and thank them.

Periodically the volunteer coordinator and the principal need to evaluate the volunteer program. To gather information teachers can be asked to respond both orally and in writing as to the effectiveness of the program. Volunteers can either be interviewed or asked to answer pertinent questions in a survey.

Informal comments and notes also provide insights and useful information about the volunteer program. Suggestion forms are another way to solicit ideas from both teachers and volunteers on how to strengthen the program.

It is important to report the results of the evaluation to the staff, volunteers and other parents. Needed adjustments in the program can be made on the evaluation results. The information can be used to publicize the program for future recruiting and to demonstrate the value of the program to those involved and to those in policy-making positions.

For a communication network to be effective, it must be responsive to community needs. Sometimes it is necessary for the principal to take a proactive stance and create a needed program. In 1980 there was a lack of child care providers within the Garden Road Elementary School attendance area. As a result there were many latchkey children in the community. Under the direction of the principal, the school implemented a fully parent paid child care program for school age children. The Extended Student Services program is now available in all of the District Elementary Schools. In 1989 enrollment exceeded 1000 students. This service is available year round and operates from 6.30 a.m. to 6.00 p.m. Students from Kindergarten through fifth grade may enroll.

Extended Student Services is designed to provide a bridge between home and school. This nonprofit, optional service offers a rich and diverse program of academic, social and recreational experiences. The staff of community resource aides is well trained to provide for the academic and social needs of elementary age children in a safe and nurturing environment. A key component is the emphasis placed on the reinforcement of the social, motor and academic skills the students are learning in the classroom. The program provides time, space, encouragement and support for developing good study habits. Time is provided for each child to complete homework assignments within a supervised environment. The program is geared toward expanding the child's world through arts and crafts projects, reading and language reinforcement, math and science extension activities. Each day, children prepare and eat nutritious snacks. When parents gather their children from the program each day, homework is completed and the child has been cared for in a comfortable environment. Parents and children are encouraged to enjoy each others' company in the evening.

General Public

Schools that communicate with the general public in some organized way enhance their chances of getting better public support, minimizing criticism and receiving assistance in educating students better. Schools should not only rely on the use of newsletters and regular articles in the local press, but should also design person-to-person programs to inform members of the community about events and activities taking place in the schools. These programs help the general public understand new educational programs, gain information about decisions made by the school district, and answer questions.

The principal should make a conscious effort to initiate closer contacts with the various community service groups and should be available to make presentations at their meetings. Often these organizations are willing to assist a school with special projects such as Reading I Fundamental book distributions, vision screening, special education field trips, and other projects related to the purposes of their organization.

Members of the business community are also often interested in education. Partners in Education and the Adopt-A-School program enable area businesses to become actively involved in Poway schools. The principal of each school locates a local business to adopt their school. Events and activities sponsored by the adopter vary from school to school. In the past, events and activities sponsored by adopters included: judging spelling bees; sponsorship of assemblies; participation in motivational reading programs; job shadowing; creation and awarding of scholarships, as well as donations to the school such as wide screen televisions, computers, furniture and funds for school projects. The District adopters also sponsor an annual Mentor Teacher recognition dinner which showcases both of these exemplary programs.

As cited by David (1988) in her report to the National Governors Association, the Poway School District operates under a decentralized management system. This is the result of a process begun by the super-intendent on his arrival in the district thirteen years ago. Each school receives virtually all of the funds it will use to operate during the year, including money for staffing and for instructional supplies. Funds allo-cated for building maintenance, food and transportation services, as well as the bulk of staff development are retained by the district.

Based upon the school enrollment each school receives a lump-sum budget for staffing purposes and implementation of the instructional program. The staffing budget is allocated in terms of Personal Staffing Units. One unit is equal to the average teacher salary plus benefits. At the elementary level, State regulations combined with union agreements on class size predetermine that the majority of the staffing budget will go to classroom teachers. However, every school has one or more staffing units over which they have total discretion. These units are to be used to effectively manage the school. One school might choose to hire several instructional aides, another a part-time music or art specialist, or obtain additional noon duty supervisors.

In addition to the staffing units, each school receives an annual general fund budget. These funds can be used to purchase instructional supplies, library books, or to pay for field trips and other school related expenses. In 1988–89, a school with 800 students received a budget of $75,000. In addition, each school also receives its share from the state-funded School Improvement Program and lottery. Each principal deter-mines the process for deciding how these funds will be spent. The degree to which teachers are involved in the school level decisions is largely dependent upon the principal. At some schools a portion of the expendi-tures is decided upon by a school-wide committee and agreed on by the entire staff. At other sites part of the budget is divided among the teachers to be spent as each teacher believes best meets the needs of the students. Each school is unique and each determines budget expenditures in a different manner.

In order to function effectively in a decentralized management sys-tem, the well organized principal must communicate clearly and effec-tively with the staff. It has been found that when teachers are involved in the decision making process, high morale exists and they describe themselves as professionals.

Internal Communication

An effective principal must work with members of the school staff to build a cooperative team. The principal needs to develop a positive attitude in each member of the staff. Not only must this attitude be present, it must be evident in their behavior. It is not enough for the principal to state that they believe in staff involvement in the decision-making process, they must act on this philosophy in their day-to-day relationships. By showing high regard for their staff this will generate mutual respect and a spirit of good will. If mutual respect is to develop within the school, the staff must perceive that the principal is sincere and honest. Principals must train themselves to be sensitive to the importance of open, honest two-way communication through their own behavior and actions.

At regular staff meetings the staff needs to be brought together to share ideas, identify instructional problems, define goals, pool resources, and coordinate services and programs. In order for staff meetings to be most productive and conducted in timely fashion it is important that agenda be well developed. In this way, time is not wasted explaining and defining facts. The staff can then get to the business of discussing and making decisions.

It is important for the principal to provide frequent staff recognition, not only for outstanding achievement, but also for the everyday services they perform in order to make school a comfortable place for everyone. This can be accomplished verbally and through informal notes. It has proven to be efficient to keep a sheet of paper for each staff member, listing the extra services and responsibilities they have assumed through-out the school year. This information is extremely useful when it is time to write commendations for the end-of-year evaluation process.

Staff members need to know they are appreciated and respected. An open door to the principal's office where they can express their sugges-tions, frustrations, or just visit, is vital for an effective internal com-munication component. In addition to notes of appreciation, people enjoy receiving birthday cards and friendly letters during vacation periods.

Strategic Planning

In order to be prepared for the future and have control over its own destiny the Poway Unified School District engages in a strategic planning process. In 1988 the district found itself at a critical juncture. It was quickly moving from a small district to a large district. Student popula-tion was increasing by 8 to 10 per cent annually. The District's student population will be over 23,000 by 1995 and 38,000 by the year 2000. The District, proud of its reputation, was committed to preserving its unique innovative qualities and at the same time meet the needs of the growing student population.

Strategic planning is more commonly associated with business rather than with education. However, the District chose to take a proactive stance and established the Strategic Planning Committee. This planning process was very different from long-range planning or forecasting, and it was much more than an attempt to anticipate the future. Through the strategic planning process, the District was able to envision the type of future it wanted and then develop the procedures and operations necessary to achieve that future.

During the 1988–89 school year the sixteen member Strategic Planning Committee held intensive planning sessions. During these sessions and with input from parents, school board members and District support staff, the committee defined the District's core values and mission statement. It now provides a clear focus and direction for the District which enables the District to take control of its destiny rather than being controlled by circumstance. The mission statement and core values not only drive District decisions, but also serve as a guide for the allocation of resources. The next phase of strategic planning involved the establishment of Critical Success Indicators. These indicators are used throughout the district to provide specific, measurable outcomes for which everyone within the District is responsible.

Mission Statement
We believe all students can learn.

Our mission is to help each student master the knowledge and develop the skills and attitudes necessary to be successful in school and society.

To fulfill our mission, we provide comprehensive K–12 programs, as well as early childhood and adult education programs, which utilize a wide variety of learning strategies, experiences, and support services to promote student learning.

Active involvement of a competent and caring staff, effective management of resources, and a safe and orderly environment are essential to our mission.

We will achieve excellence in all we do.
Core Values

Excellence in All We Do
We are committed to:
> our collective contribution to the learning process
> high levels of performance

continuous improvement
pride in all aspects of the organization.

Student Learning
We are committed to all our students learning; therefore, we will help each student, to the best of his or her ability, master the knowledge and develop the skills necessary to be successful in school and society.

Competent and Caring Staff
We are committed to selecting, developing, and supporting the best possible staff which will:
understand and contribute to the learning process
perform at a high level
care about students
respect others, and
act in an ethical manner.

Active Staff Participation
We are committed to extensive and appropriate involvement of staff to promote healthier, more effective organization.

Safe, Orderly, and Attractive Environment
We are committed to providing and maintaining a safe, orderly, and attractive environment which promotes productivity and stimulates learning.

Effective Management of Resources
We are committed to aggressively seeking, effectively managing, and creatively using our resources to achieve our mission. These resources include students, staff, school board, parents, community finances, time, facilities and equipment.

Elementary School Survey Questions

1   Are you satisfied with your child's *academic progress* toward advancement to the next grade level?
2   Do you feel the *reading program* meets your child's needs?
3   Do you feel the *math program* meets your child's needs?
4   Do you feel your child is receiving good classroom *instruction*?
5   Do you feel the progress reports and parent conferences give you an adequate *report* on the *progress* of your child?
6   Do you feel there is reasonable *discipline* maintained in your child's classroom?
7   Do you feel the *rules* and *regulations* of the school are enforced uniformly and fairly?

8   Are you satisfied with the *quality* of *homework* assignments?

9   Do you feel the *amount* of *homework* assigned is:

(a) [ ] About right?   (b) [ ] Too much?   (c) [ ] Too little?

10   Do you feel you are being adequately *informed* about the *plans* and *programs* at your child's school?

11   Do you feel that your child receive *help* from the *teachers* when it is requested?

12   Do you feel that the school handles *attendance* problems satisfactorily?

13   Are you made to feel *welcome* at your child's school?

14   Do you feel there is good school-parent *communication*?

15   Do you feel you have adequate opportunities to have a *voice* in *school decisions* that affect you and your child?

16   Do you favor *year-round* school to ease overcrowding?

17   Do you feel your school has a *safe, orderly, and attractive* environment?

18   Do you feel your child's school is *free* from drugs and alcohol?

19   Do you feel the *PTA* performs an effective function at your child's school?

20   Does *your child like school?*

21   *Overall*, are you generally satisfied with your child's school?

22   Should the Poway Unified School District consider *changing its name* to reflect all the areas it serves?

23   What are the main sources of your *information* about your child's school?

(a)   [ ] School/PTA Newsletters   (f)   [ ] Newspaper
(b)   [ ] Your child   (g)   [ ] Neighbors
(c)   [ ] PTA meetings   (h)   [ ] School Advisory
(d)   [ ] Parent-teacher conferences   Council
(e)   [ ] Custodians, secretaries,   (i)   [ ] Teachers and
             bus drivers, etc.   administrators

Do you have any comments?

Middle School Survey Questions

1   Do you feel your student is being *well prepared* to enter high school?

2   Do you feel the *reading program* meets your student's needs?

3   Do you feel the *math program* meets your student's needs?

4   Do you feel your student is receiving good classroom *instruction*?

5   Do you feel the progress reports and parent conferences give you an adequate *report* on the *progress* of your student?

6   Do you feel there is a reasonable *discipline* maintained in your student's classroom?

7   Do you feel the *rules* and *regulations* of the school are enforced uniformly and fairly?
8   Are you satisfied with the *quality* of *homework* assignments?
9   Do you feel the *amount* of *homework* assigned is:

(a) [   ] About right?   (b) [   ] Too much?   (c) [   ] Too little?

10   Do you feel you are being adequately *informed* about the *plans* and *programs* at your student's school?
11   Do you feel that your student receives *help* from the *teachers* when it is requested?
12   Do you feel that the school handles *attendance* problems satisfactorily?
13   Are you made to feel *welcome* at your student's school?
14   Do you feel there is good school–parent *communication*?
15   Do you feel you have adequate opportunities to have a *voice* in *school decisions* that affect you and your student?
16   Do you favor *year-round* school to ease overcrowding?
17   Do you feel your school has a *safe, orderly, and attractive* environment?
18   Do you feel your student's school is *free* from drugs and alcohol?
19   Do you feel the school has an adequate *extra-curricular activity program*?
20   Do you feel the school provides effective *counseling* and *guidance*?
21   Does *your student like school*?
22   *Overall*, are you generally satisfied with your student's school?
23   Should the Poway Unified School District consider *changing its name* to reflect all the areas it serves?
24   What are the main sources of your *information* about your student's school?

(a)   [   ] School/PTA Newsletters   (f)   [   ] Newspaper
(b)   [   ] Your child   (g)   [   ] Neighbors
(c)   [   ] PTA meetings   (h)   [   ] School Advisory
(d)   [   ] Parent-teacher conferences   Council
(e)   [   ] Custodians, secretaries,   (i)   [   ] Teachers and
      bus drivers, etc.   administrators

Do you have any comments?

High School Survey Questions

1   Do you feel the *academic standards* of the school are satisfactory?
2   Do you feel your student is receiving good classroom *instruction*?
3   Do you feel the progress reports and parent conferences give you an adequate *report* on the *progress* of your student?
4   Do you feel there is reasonable *discipline* maintained in your student's classroom?

5 Do you feel the *rules* and *regulations* of the school are enforced uniformly and fairly?
6 Are you satisfied with the *quality* of *homework* assignments?
7 Do you feel the *amount* of *homework* assigned is:

(a) [   ] About right?   (b) [   ] Too much?   (c) [   ] Too little?

8 Do you feel you are being adequately *informed* about the *plans* and *programs* at your student's school?
9 Do you feel that your student receives *help* from the *teachers* when it is requested?
10 Do you feel that the school handles *attendance* problems satisfactorily?
11 Are you made to feel *welcome* at your student's school?
12 Do you feel there is good school-parent *communication*?
13 Do you feel you have adequate opportunities to have a *voice* in *school decisions* that affect you and your student?
14 Do you favor *year-round* school to ease overcrowding?
15 Do you feel your school has a *safe, orderly, and attrative* environment?
16 Do you feel your student's school is *free* from drugs and alcohol?
17 Are you satisfied with the *process* used for students to *select classes*?
18 Are you satisfied with the *course offerings* provided at the high school?
19 Do you feel the *library* and *media center* meet the needs of the student?
20 Do you feel the school has an adequate *extra-curricular activity program*?
21 Do you feel the school provides effective *counseling* and *guidance*?
22 Do you feel the school offers an effective *college preparatory curriculum*?
23 Do you feel the school provides effective *career* and *vocational education*?
24 Does *your student like school*?
25 *Overall,* are you generally satisfied with your student's school?
26 Should the Poway Unified School District consider *changing its name* to reflect all the areas it serves?
27 What are the main sources of your *information* about your student's school?

(a) [   ] School/PTA Newsletters   (f) [   ] Newspaper
(b) [   ] Your child   (g) [   ] Neighbors
(c) [   ] PTA meetings   (h) [   ] School Advisory
(d) [   ] Parent-teacher conferences   Council
(e) [   ] Custodians, secretaries, (i) [   ] Teachers and
          bus drivers, etc.   administrators

Do you have any comments?

Key Points

1 It is incumbent upon the principal to be aware of all his constituencies because of the impact they have on the organizational system.
2 A critical aspect to understanding and applying proactive decision making rests in strong communication systems. These systems are developed and maintained by members of the school and community but coordinated by the principal.
3 There must be a strong and carefully planned integration between the community needs and expectations and the school activities and programs in order to create a total learning environment. This speaks to the development of a holistic educational approach.
4 Appropriate and reinforced staff development procedures must be institutionalized to provide school personnel with opportunities for personal and professional growth.
5 There must be a school vision that represents the entire school community and reflects its philosophy and future goals.

Discussion Questions

1 What are the initial steps necessary in order for a principal to create a positive school climate?
2 Who are the important members of the school community that should be involved in decision making?
3 What is the role of the business community regarding curriculum development?
4 How can community service be incorporated into curriculum developments?
5 State five leadership traits demonstrated in this section and how they were evidenced by the principal in the organization's objectives?

References

DAVID, J.L. (1988) *Restructuring in Progress: Lessons From Pioneering Districts*, Paper for National Governors' Association.
EPSTEIN, J.L. (1986) 'Parents' reactions to teacher practices of parent involvement', *Elementary School Journal*, **86**, pp. 277–93.
EPSTEIN, J.L. (1988) 'How do we improve programs for parents involvement', *Educational Horizons*, **66**, 2, pp. 57–9.
GORDON, I. (1978) *What does Research Say About the Effects of Parent*

Andrew E. Dubin

Involvement on Schooling? Paper for the Annual Meeting of the Association for Supervision and Curriculum Development.

RICH, D. (1986) 'Helping parents help their children learn', *Elementary School Journal*, **86**, p. 276.
WALBERG, H.J., PASCHAL, R.A. and WEINSTEIN, T. (1985) 'Homework's powerful effects on learning', *Educational Leadership*, **47**, pp. 76–80.

Chapter 3

Interviews with Chief Executive Officers: The Role of the Principal

Introduction

In this chapter we find the philosophies and experiences of four chief executive officers as they perceive the role of the principal as a proactive decision maker. In addition, each comments on the impact he believes the education reform movement will have on our schooling enterprise. The CEOs approach the various questions quite differently since they come from different backgrounds and assume different professional roles. Yet, what makes their feedback so interesting, useful and important is that their orientations will have a direct bearing on the role the principal assumes.

For example, Ramon Cortines, Superintendent of San Francisco Unified School District, sees the principal as the catalyst for change, ever searching for ways to improve conditions. At one point when describing the principal as a risk taker, he states that a principal '. . . is not the individual who has arrived. They are constantly reaching for the brass ring, perfecting, fine tuning, not only themselves, but providing the same opportunities for others'. He also states that he must be creative in his commitment to excellence in education. He clearly identifies the principal as 'leader', always aware of the entire picture and being 'all things to all people'. In this way the principal can be the effective proactive decision maker. He also emphasizes and identifies the information sources utilized by effective principals as being people-centered; critical information location and utilization is realized within the school constituency, that is, faculty/staff and the greater community.

While Cortines speaks of proactive decision making from both the educational CEO's perspective as well as a seasoned experiential base, Jerry Hume's response is based on a CEO's management in private enterprise perspective and a private sector recipient of our school's product, that is, the student. Hume identified the principal as being the leader, essentially the same as the role he has played as CEO of Basic

American Foods through the years. He did see the environment changing significantly and thus having an important impact on the principal. Because the student population has undergone enormous change, it is crucial the principal and schools be responsive. Yet, he ardently asserts that the schools failed to respond. He cites such examples as the limited utilization of new technologies, pedagogues mired in antiquated techniques and the structure itself failing to adapt to the needs of a modern society. He discusses incentive processes he felt to be highly effective in developing career opportunities for teachers, accountability procedures to reward and/or sanction schools dependent upon performance and student evaluation strategies that would ensure that learning would take place.

Dean Henrietta Schwartz, Dean of the School of Education at San Francisco State University offers a University CEO's perspective on the proactive role of the principal. Dean Schwartz defines the difference in proactive and reactive decision making. The idenfication and utilization of information sources is also analyzed and reviewed as she cites her administrative experiences in the school system in Chicago. She comments on the education reform movement and what impact it could have on our schools in the future with specific application to the principal. Her views are both research and experientially based, providing a rich and complete analysis.

In the first of the interviews, President Corrigan provides his views of effective decision making as perceived from a post-secondary administrative point of view. His understanding and input regarding the principal's role in effective decision making in a K-12 setting are illuminating since he offers a rich experiential background from his work in Boston as well. His comments on proactive decision making as it relates to the higher education arena, though, are extremely provocative and insightful. Shared decision making, understanding the political arena endemic to organizational settings, the role of values as it impacts decision making and process, are some of the focal points of his interview.

Section One: Dr. Robert A. Corrigan, President, San Francisco State University

A native of Springfield, Massachusetts, Dr. Corrigan received his BA in American Civilization from Brown University in 1957 and his MA (1959) and PhD (1967) in that field from the University of Pennsylvania. He has published widely on the poet Ezra Pound, issues facing urban, public universities, and Black American literature. As Chancellor at the University of Massachusetts, Boston, he brought its diverse student population into close partnership with the city of Boston, forming institutes to deal with race relations, water pollution and gaining scholarships and other support from Boston businesses. During his tenure *Time* magazine identified UMASS Boston as one of nine 'Hot Colleges on the Climb'. Dr. Corrigan was appointed president of San Francisco State on September 17, 1988.

Dr. Dubin: What do you find the role to be of the principal in the wave of education reform?

President Corrigan: I have become convinced, as I think have many other people in post-secondary education have, that school-based management is something that needs to be instituted. I think in Boston, in particular, which was a very tough, heavily, centralized administration, that the people who had charge of the buildings, so to speak, the principals and headmasters, felt very frustrated by their inability to make the kinds of decisions in important areas such as curriculum and choice of teachers. Their inability, for example, simply to get repair work done in order to create a more appropriate place for students to study was very frustrating ... So I come to San Francisco as somebody who has already been sensitized to the issue of principals having a major role in the decision-making process. Now, if I can add to that, in the debate as I understand it to be taking place in San Francisco, there is an additional component that I find equally compelling ... the involvement of teachers themselves, in the decision-making process. I've often thought that teaching may be the only 'profession' in which the professionals are treated like a blue collar class, and I mean no disparagement of blue collar workers. What I'm getting at is the extent to which, unlike other professionals, teachers often times lack the respect, the compensation, the sense of dignity and the sense of being involved in the control of their own lives and environment. And, insofar as we limit the opportunity of teachers to control choice of text, to be in charge of what happens in the classroom, to be able to order their lives in a way that makes them feel professionally in control, I believe we will continue to have a problem with the morale of teachers. I believe in the importance of principals sharing authority with superintendents and boards of education. I also think it is important that principals themselves become comfortable with sharing increasing amounts of authority and responsibility with classroom teachers.

Dubin: How would you see the role of the principal different from the past five years or ten years? Do you see differences and in what way?

Corrigan: Well, as I answer this, you have to remember that my experiences are entirely with post-secondary education. It's more in the role of a concerned citizen or as somebody who as chancellor or president has interacted with the schools, that I form any judgment at all. Secondly, I am limited by having had relatively close observation of only one major school district in this period of time. I would say that in Boston, which is the city with which I had the most recent and detailed experience, that a combination of factors, beginning some fifteen years ago, tended to conspire against the principal in terms of his or her ability to be involved in major decision making. There was an increased concentration of authority in the hands of the superintendent, a concern on the part of the electorate that the school committee itself had to be more involved in micro-managing the schools, because of community suspicion of professional educators. The suspicion was of principals in general, who were perceived as part of the old boy system, a White male orthodoxy, that was not sensitive or responsive to the needs of a largely ethnic minority school population. To add to this, we had in Boston a renewed interest on the part of the business community in the effective management of the schools; that is the pairing of university and colleges with the schools in partnerships between the university and a local company working with the school. I think all of this added to an increased set of pressures on the principal. Finally, I would add that the powerful role of the unions, along with the courts taking such an interest in public schools, meant that the frustrations school committees and superintendents had about their ability to run the schools, was transmitted down the ladder. Perhaps the single most important thing that happened in Boston while I was there was Judge Garath's decision to return to the superintendent of schools the authority to run the system. That superintendent, Laval Wilson, in turn decided that he would empower the principals and headmasters to have a much more direct and powerful role in administration. So, over a period of fifteen years of decline in power and authority for the principal, in the last year or two I feel that the principal has re-emerged in a position of significance within a school system. That's a layman's view of it.

Dubin: Let me ask you about your general feelings about proactive and pre-emptive decision making. What does that mean to you and how do you practice that?

Corrigan: I suspect what's meant by the question is, that administrators who are sensitive to what's going on in the environment can often times anticipate what issues are likely to be. Therefore, they are able to make decisions that are either responsive to the concerns out there or because they may at an appropriate time, actually keep an unpleasant set of circumstances from coming together and creating problems. Recently, I was asked to participate in a class at Berkeley on presidential administrations. The text the class had been reading had a chapter in it about cybernetic administration, which I thought was an interesting phrase. Many years ago I was an avid reader of science fiction, so that on my previous job, after I had it for a number of years, the concept of cybernetics used to come to mind. You may remember the science fiction stories in which a brain, cut out of a human body was hooked up to a vast computer producing an extraordinary, powerful sort of force. On my best days at the University of Massachusetts at Boston, I felt a little bit like that brain tied into the system because the communication flow was so good that I felt, not so much in charge in a power sense, but in tune with what was going on. So, the decisions I made, the things I got involved with, were almost instinctive in terms of knowing the institution as well I did. That's not a feeling I have yet about San Francisco State because I'm still too new here. My point would be that often I was able to anticipate issues or problems because of the communication flow and therefore could make a decision well in advance of a crisis. The other part of this is that I believe higher education administration tends to be increasingly in the hands of people who are reluctant to make decisions, who turn to committees and advisory groups for study and consultation; endless study and endless consultation. It's one of the reasons why I think we are ineffective and as slow to change. I'm not advocating a kind of military, proactive arbitrary sort of administrative style, which is characteristic of very few college or university presidents. But I am delegated the authority by the trustees and the chancellor to lead this institution and I therefore believe I have the responsibility to make the best possible decisions on the basis of the evidence available. Sometimes those decisions are going to be made in the face of much opposition and be responded to very critically. I think presidents who try to satisfy every constituency or respond or make decisions only when encouraged to do so by planning committees or consultants are depriving universities and colleges of the leadership they were hired to provide. Obviously, I characterize myself as someone who tends to be proactive, as opposed to reactive, in the decision-making process.

Dubin: In the context of that answer, you responded that you had a very strong intuitive sense to anticipating problems because you were so connected to the system. Could you tell me a little about the types of sources you were so closely connected to in order to provide you with the necessary information?

Corrigan: A good president is someone who gets out of the office as much as possible, a person who is in direct contact with the faculty and the leadership of the faculty but doesn't restrict himself or herself only to the leadership group, but seeks opportunities for interaction with the entire faculty. Similarly perhaps on a lesser set of issues, not less important but fewer, a president is also one who is sensitive to the needs of students. But, again, it is through formal meetings with student leadership or just simply casual conversations, by reading the student press, being conscious of the letters that come from students that the president gains vital information. No matter whether I'm the president or chancellor, I have always insisted that every piece of mail come across my desk, no matter how insignificant or irrelevant it may appear to what ordinarily concerns me. I read everything. As I said, I try to be open and as receptive as possible to all groups within the university. Finally, I would add to the internal process the importance of being externally involved; being active in the community, having a sense of how the institution is viewed, anticipating what the overall issues are likely to be that will effect the institution and learning from your experiences is extremely important.

Dubin: I understand completely. Now, with respect to the use of information, you've mentioned many different areas. Could you speak to your experience in the use of technology and how it has facilitated that proactive decision-making process?

Corrigan: In a very limited way because as you can see by looking around this office, I'm not much of a user of technology myself. I'm much more of a people-oriented administrator. The extent to which technology has been useful and important is dependent on how the people who work for me are able to gather more data, analyze that data and present me with alternatives for decision making. If I can sound a somewhat pessimistic note, I think that too many people in higher education have been caught up in the romance of the hardware and the software and have forgotten that, ultimately, human beings must make decisions that affect other human beings. A decision that can appear very logical when dictated by the data that's produced by the technology, is not necessarily the best for the institution. I guess the simple answer to your question is, the extent to which my advisors are better informed about the facts, defines my use of technology.

Dubin: Could you draw distinctions between those in decision-making positions in a private enterprise as opposed to public education? How they go about making decisions, how they interact with people, different types of leadership traits, characteristics.

Corrigan: I don't know that you can generalize and I don't know that any college or university president is in a position to comment with intelligence on how people in the private sector function ... I take it you mean private sector business CEOs. There is as much difference amongst companies and businesses as there is amongst colleges and universities. But, there do seem to be some generalizations that you can arrive at. There's far more shared authority in the public college or university. Not only is there more shared authority but often times there is a great deal of accountability that constrains the president or chancellor, but not always the authority to go along with that accountability. My impression is that in the private sector administrators are held accountable but they are also given authority. If they fail then their services are dispensed with but they're given all of the authority generally that they need to do their job. In this job I have a faculty senate, faculty union, student organizations, and staff organizations and unions. I have deans, department chairs. I have cabinet level people. All of these people assume, quite correctly that they have some right to be consulted and listened to in the decision-making process. I share my authority in decision making off the campus with a chancellor, vice chancellors, a board of trustees, a post-secondary education commission, a volunteer presidents' advisory council, a

governor, with a legislature, and with key staff people working for legis-
lators, such as budget analysts. Twice a week I have a campus newspaper
that comes out to advise me on or second guess the decisions I do make. I
doubt there are many private sector CEOs that have to deal with the
complexity of the constraints on individual decision making than the head
of major public university or college has to deal with. I don't know
whether that's a response to your question.

Dubin: No, that was a good response, an interesting response. In the
light of all these constituents you've just mentioned that there obviously
is a need, one you identify philosophically, if not certainly in practice, to
incorporate others in that whole process. Yet you also mention that the
process of shared decision making can be very time consuming and can
also be a real inhibitor. Can you identify a moment where you have had
to make a decision that either traditionally or within the context of that
decision, could have involved other committee work, but you felt that the
better decision would have been, and was, to act more autonomously?

Corrigan: I'm concerned about executive leadership and it's very important to make it quite clear what you stand for as the president or chancellor. You must take every opportunity to articulate to a larger community
what the values are that you share and to what extent these values you
believe in should be institutional values. Search committees, for example,
spend a lot of time ultimately choosing among the numbers of people
who all qualify for the position of president. In that selection, they are
looking for the largest commonality of values. It won't be a complete
overlap obviously between, for argument's sake, what the faculty leadership wants and what the new president believes in. But the extent to
which there's a major overlap it is going to make executive decision
making a lot easier. So, in part, communication is a sort of a two-way
street. Often when difficult decisions are made, they're made in the
context of people sharing the value system that characterizes them. As far
as a decision of the kind that you asked about, i.e., the interweave of
autonomous and shared decision making, I'll provide a personal example.
When I was interviewed for the Presidency, much emphasis was given to
the campus need for a real political constituency, for a community base,
the need to be better known in the community, concern that the campus
was too dependent upon the central office for its representation in the
state legislature, concern for our lack of political sophistication and so on.
Shortly after I took office faculty teachers began to go out of their way,
as is customary, to ensure I made the acquaintance of influential people
who could help move the university forward and to rewrite the master
plan for higher education. I thought the signals were quite clear that
people thought that one of the ways in which I could make major strides
forward in our ability to relate better to the city, the Capital and the
community in general, was to add a particular person to my staff. I spent
about three months studying the situation before deciding that the faculty

was absolutely right and that I needed to proceed in this way. I strategized in this manner, floated various balloons, as is my wont, in a number of places on the campus and I received genuinely positive responses. What then absolutely perplexed me was the secondary set of responses, from a variety of places on the campus, that I should conduct a national search that would produce as a finalist the person everyone agreed should be hired. I relied upon my own instincts and my own sense of the appropriateness of certain appointments and made it over the objections of a number of people, many of whom I respect, who are concerned by process. I think one of the important elements of being an effective administrator is your ability both to respect process but also to recognize the times that a slavish adherence to process will keep you from accomplishing what needs to be accomplished. In this instance I thought it was a perfect example of how one should go after the substance and ignore the process. Over the next several months I had nothing but very positive comments regarding this personnel decision.

Dubin: The focus and concern in some circles about the issue of choice is something that is a moving force in our K–12 schools. As you know, choice refers to parents having the right to withdraw their children from schools they feel are ineffective and inadequate in providing a viable education. What impact do you feel choice would have on K–12 schools and specifically in urban centers?

Corrigan: I served for a year and a half on a committee in the Boston public schools, charged with the responsibility by the superintendent with coming up with a system that would provide more choice for parents. I became very sensitive to the issue as a a result of comparing my own experiences as a parent. Between us, my wife and I had put five kids through school and, because generally of our middle-class situation, noticed the choice that we had with regard to where we lived, even in a community that had neighborhood schools ... the options that were available to us when compared to the situation of parents in the inner city. Often times parents or parent, in most instances, who lived in public housing, no matter how vitally interested that parent might be about the quality of the education the child received, was unaware, or unable, to make important decisions about the education of their children. That problem was exacerbated in Boston. Let me very deliberately talk about Black parents as opposed to White parents because choice is often discussed in terms of White parents. As I've suggested to you, as a result of court order busing, even Black parents, who would manage by virtue of buying or renting in a particular neighborhood, in what had been a predominantly Black community, found themselves having to accept the fact that their children could not go down the street to the school that they had chosen to be their children's school. The children were being bused out of that neighborhood into an environment that was quite hostile to their children.... Indeed, bused into schools that had been predominantly historically White, that didn't necessarily provide the quality of education nor the role models that they were looking for because of the nature of the teacher population. Then to exacerbate that problem they discovered that their children, often times because of the GEO codes, were being bused out of a Black neighborhood into another Black neighborhood on the other side of the city. They were bused into schools that might not be as good, where the role models might be there but then didn't have the neighborhood and community support. And so, questions of being able to participate in after school activities, of going to school with people who are also your friends and neighbors, all the things we tend to value about a neighborhood school, were being denied them. So this made me be very sensitive to the whole issue. In part, I saw it as a class issue, because in point of fact, suburban parents have a lot of choice. The more money you have, the more choice you're likely to have for your children. The people who have the least amount of choice are those people who are poor and live in urban neighborhoods. So I think I've become much more attuned to the need to provide working-class families, Black or White with more choice then they had had historically. I did, in fact, work on the plan that was ultimately adopted in Boston, that allowed the city to insure that to the extent that the schools were desegregated, within certain sectors, the parents would be able to send their children to elementary and middle schools of their choosing.

Dubin: I see. There's another issue that essentially speaks to the perpetuation of the type of school conditions that tend not to provide the kind of support that under-represented children require.

Corrigan: Yes. For example, the choice within the county as opposed to just simply within the city or the Berkeley proposal which would merge private schools with public schools.

Dubin: Yes, also the concern that if parents are not alerted to the types of school conditions, i.e., faculty, students, materials, safety and so forth, that is essential information necessary for them to make an appropriate choice, we'd be creating a greater problem, i.e., segmentation, with the choice then with eliminating it.

Corrigan: Yes. Your choice has to be an informed one. For example, the typical phenomenon of middle-class suburban communities, the PTA, is a mechanism which allows middle-class people to be more involved in their schools than relatively less educated people who are working or disengaged from their school or don't have the free time in the cities. In Boston again, part of court order busing had required that there be parent councils. The court actually ruled that parents be paid, as if it were a job, to be involved in the schools. But even given that situation, what we discovered was that parents in inner-city schools, on the whole, were not as knowledgeable of, or concerned about, or involved in what was going on in the schools. A lot of the pressure for choice was coming from very selected neighborhoods within Boston, enclaves of middle-class and

79

upper-middle-class White parents who were striving for more choice for themselves and were less concerned about the choice factor for the working-class parents. It became a difficult issue. I would argue, as I think you are, that the choice in itself means nothing unless it's informed choice. But I don't know what the answer is in terms of providing information that they can have and work with. I'm watching the Chicago situation with fascination with the regard to school councils. As I understand it, all you need to do, to be, is eighteen years old. It will be very interesting to see how that works itself out.

Dubin: In one of the interviews I conducted with a private sector individual, he identified very strongly with choice and felt, in the same context, that private enterprise is accountable for its products and if the product is not received well by the consumer then it will cease to exist in the market place. By the same token, if schools are no longer able to function effectively they should no longer exist. But the question ...?

Corrigan: We had that argument in Boston. We should give complete freedom of choice to all parents and then judge the quality of the schools and the quality of the principals on the basis of where the better students went. To some extent, I would tie this with the opening discussion we had. A principal must, in fact, control the entire educational environment; choice of teachers, choice of curriculum, choice of text, etc. In Boston, for example, the same basal reader often had to be used in every single second grade in the community. A principal could not hire and fire his or her own faculty. Union seniority rules prevailed, so often times the choice of faculty in the school would be determined on/by conditions over which the principal had no control. I guess, in the best of all possible worlds, I'd be willing to go along with the private sector notion which is essentially a kind of Darwinian one. But we have to do a lot more in terms of the basic support for independent decision making on the part of the principal for that to work. Outside of private prep schools, with which I've had a limited amount of experience, my suspicion is that the bureaucracies of public school systems, at least urban school systems, are going to inhibit our ability to provide that kind of, both, positive and negative conditioning for the whole alleged decision making in that regard.

Dubin: Can the analogy be applied to schools, i.e., if the product fails is it discontinued? But schools can't nor do populations of kids go away! If indeed you have choice, the 'aware' parents can identify the schools that would be most appropriate, and others will not be able to. There are those who feel that a whole class system might develop!

Corrigan: Well, take the Minnesota example. Politicians in Boston got fascinated with the decision that was reached in Minnesota that the state would support a voucher system through which essentially an inner-city kid could go anyplace within reason. The president of the Massachusetts senate proposed in successive years of the legislature that Massachusetts adopt such a voucher system. And by the way, we also had the head of a major Catholic university in town, Boston College supporting vouchers, as well as the president of Boston University. Many of us felt that strategy would be the absolute final kiss of death to the Boston public schools because virtually the last of the minority parents who had any appreciation at all or understanding of how the schools work, would opt to take advantage of the voucher system. Their kids would end up going to suburban schools and all that would be left in Boston would be the really at-risk students who didn't have parents or support systems that could help them. Boston went from 85,000 students in the public school system to 55,000 students from roughly 1974 to 1985. During that period of time, the White population in the parochial schools within Boston grew to a number where they outnumbered the White students in the public schools in Boston. The most troublesome phenomenon that we were seeing after 1985, from the point of view of those of us concerned about the future cost to public schools, was that Black parents, not Roman Catholics, were increasingly electing to send their children to the parochial schools. You know I don't have any empirical data to suggest that these students were better students, better prepared students than the ones who remain behind. Nonetheless, the following resulted: first we had White kids going to the suburbs, followed by Operation Exodus, as it was first called, that bused something like 2000 Black students a year to suburban schools. Then we had students, Black and White, going into the parochial schools. We had the exam high schools; four of the high schools out of the eighteen high schools in Boston were exam schools. So that we had all these different institutionally supported activities that took away the best of the students from the rest of the schools. If you were a student at one of the regional, non-exam schools in Boston the quality of your education was influenced by the overall quality of the students who were in class with you. Again, it's an interesting debate, because on the one hand, yes, individuals ought to have the right to do best by their own children. But how do you maintain a first rate public school system in the face of that?

Dubin: Could you summarize what you consider to be the most pressing issues that principals in the K-12 setting might be facing in 1990 and beyond?

Corrigan: I am not really qualified to make that projection. From my point of view, as I have talked to principals, the overwhelming frustration they have is the extent to which they are being asked to address a whole set of community concerns that are not necessarily of an educational nature. They have often become the replacements for the church and the family, insofar as they have to deal with goals and values. Secondly, they are being asked to provide an education for an increasingly disadvantaged school population without the resources to do it. Again, it's an example of being held accountable without being given the authority and resources to do the job. We have put so much of a burden on our public schools in America, certainly the urban schools which I know best. It seems to me an almost impossible situation. We are making so many demands and providing so little in the way of authority and resources.

Key Points

1 Identifying and involving your community membership in discussion making is a characteristic of proactive decision making.
2 Use of technology, e.g., data collection, spread sheets, etc., is one variable in a proactive decision maker's arsenal. This type of information can be provided to him through his subordinates.
3 A CEO is hired because of his background, expertise in the field, methods of decision making and personal value system.
4 A principal as CEO must be provided with the autonomy to be proactive at the school site. He must be given license to hire appropriate personnel, manage the budget and develop curriculum.

Discussion Questions

1 What information sources are identified and utilized in his decision making?
2 How does he define proactive and reactive decision making?
3 In what ways does he define the educational reform movement?
4 Would you think there are common themes regarding the education reform movement that all CEOs identify as critically important? What themes does he address?
5 What do you feel would be the advantage and disadvantage in a business CEO's leadership applied to the educational enterprise and vice-versa?

Section Two: Ramon Cortines, Superintendent, San Francisco Unified School District

Ramon Cortines has spent his professional life working to better California's public educational system. His accomplishments demonstrate that public education can meet the tremendous challenges brought on by growing diversity and other fundamental changes in our society. A native San Franciscan, educated in California, Cortines has served since 1965 in four of the state's school districts as a teacher at the elementary, middle and high school levels and as an administrator. As superintendent of three major school districts, he has demonstrated his skills as a unifier, able to bring together disparate segments of a community. In

Pasadena and San José he developed and implemented desegregation plans dubbed 'symbols of success' which have since been copied in a number of other school districts. In San Francisco, Cortines heads one of the most ethnically diverse school districts in the nation. Minorities constitute some 85 per cent of the public school population in the city, compared with a statewide total of 49 per cent. His commitment to public K–12 education in California is an inspiration to colleagues in the California State University committed to public higher education and to the preparation of teachers and administrators, and to the students, especially minority students.

Dr. Dubin: What is the role of the principal in the wave of educational reform?

Superintendent Cortines: I believe the principal is still the leader. They can empower, involve and encourage participation. They can bring people along, create new ideas, and offer suggestions. It takes an individual to do that and I think that is the role of the principal. I have some problems, however, with the way the principalship is being used in the wave of reform. There is a tendency now to view the principal more as a parti-cipator and less that of a leader. I believe the principal should encourage a participative environment with his staff, but the primary role of the principal is that of the leader and he/she needs to know when to throw the ball. That does not mean that when someone else assumes a position of leadership for a period of time or in a particular subject area that the principal's leadership role is diminished. The principal can see the big picture. They know what their staff is doing and for what purpose and can coordinate their activities into a cohesive unit. There just has to be somebody in charge.

Dubin: As you reflect on your administrative experiences, how did you develop the sense of cohesion within your faculty?

Cortines: I look back to the days in the early sixties when I was a principal in a school that just had a very major racial riot, Pasadena High School with a student body of 3200. I was the assistant superintendent in the board and the superintendent asked me to go and take it for a while. I remember that it had a strong support administration, a strong depart-ment chair, a lot of parent involvement, students that were concerned and engaged in learning, and that it had a large participation in co-curricular activities, but it needed somebody to put it together. I remember that was a campus of forty acres, and because of the nervousness of everyone fol-lowing the riot I used to walk it every day and put my head into the room of every class. I did that for almost three months. It is interesting that years later teachers, students and parents comment to me that my leadership decision to settle the place down really made the difference. I made that decision based on an intuitive hunch. Another time I was named principal at a school because it was in the throes of losing its accreditation. The staff complained about the lack of motivation and self-discipline on the part of their students and how that never used to be a problem. Extreme lethargy had set in as well as a lack of purpose.

Dubin: In other words, although you agree that a shared decision making approach is desirable, the leadership role is still expected, appreciated and required?

Cortines: I have always felt that instruction is the hub of everything that goes on within a school. While I am a generalist, it is my responsibility to see that we put the spotlight on instruction, curriculum development and evaluation rather than complaining and romanticizing about the 'good old days'. The role of the leader is to bring out the talent within that school community and direct it in productive ways. It takes an individual to do that. That has not changed in the thirty one years I have been in the business. I remember my first principal talking with me about leadership because I was a good first year teacher. His evaluation to me was if you are very patient, very patient, and then he underlined patient for the third time, Cortines will create miracles in his classroom. He went onto say that in the evaluation process that I was really exerting leadership and modeling it for the sixth graders in my class. But for me he was modeling leadership by providing me the rope and yanking it when appropriate. If I made a contribution it was partly because of his early yanking on my rope or allowing me all I needed. That is individual leadership. So I don't think it has changed. If anything I think it is more needed now and I am not sure that we are training individuals to assume that responsibility which includes understanding and managing the complexities that today's children or young people bring with them, e.g., the various kinds of lifestyles, the lack of learning readiness, amount of parental support, etc. The principal should also know the cadre of teachers that are needed in a school such as the balance of older, middle-aged and young teachers, or the balance of specialists to generalists, or those who are interdisciplinary to those who are cloistered by their academic parameters. All of that is needed within a school. It takes somebody to understand that and to know that. It takes somebody who is knowledgeable of education theory and practice and has an intuitive touch to put it together and orchestrate the whole school community, whether it be a small school — elementary, middle or senior high school — or a very large school, whether it be in a suburban, rural, or inner city setting. It takes an individual that understands that even though they have reached a measure of success and are now designated as an 'educational/manager/leader', that they remain committed to personal growth, recognizing life and learning as a dynamic process. The educational leader, the principal, is not an individual that has arrived. They are constantly reaching for the brass ring, perfecting, fine tuning, not only themselves, but providing the same opportunities for others.

Dubin: What would you say a significant difference is between a proactive decision maker and a reactive one?

Cortines: A proactive decision maker reminds me of an old army term, 'observational awareness'. They are constantly aware of what is happening around them. They are aware of the student population and how it is changing. They are aware of the socio-economic, cultural and ethnic dynamics that are active within a community. Let me give you an example. When I was in San José and there was an economic downturn, we had a rash of thefts by students in our upper-middle-class schools. One principal did not understand it. Another principal not only understood it, he anticipated it. Before the thefts began he raised the issue of security in his school and urged students to be extra careful and keep their lockers locked, and so on. He understood how the dynamics of the economic downturn of the community were going to affect that school. The individual that is reactive is often so preoccupied with things other than their direct responsibility — the school community — namely concern with how an incident may reflect on their reputation, management, or leadership style. They are constantly responding after the fact, reacting to situations — issuing documents, orders, making pronouncements. If the same energy would be directed before the incidents there would not have been the same problems.

Dubin: Do you feel that leadership style is a part of that proactive or reactive posture?

Cortines: The issue, I believe, is not reactive versus proactive, but how one maintains and furthers a proactive leadership style. It is easy to blame our failures and inadequacies on the downtown office. What we need to do is develop a process where one is professionally stimulated in such a way that one is always on the cutting edge. Complacency, I believe, breeds a reactive atmosphere. I think I have always been proactive and it goes back to observational awareness which I alluded to earlier.

Dubin: What about risk — is not a proactive position one that will likely be more error prone?

Cortines: Being proactive does not mean, however, that you don't make mistakes in trying to deal with issues and situations before they become major problems. When you do make a wrong decision as a proactive individual I think it fine tunes your process. It makes you look inward, do research, read, calculate and analyze and, therefore, is professionally stimulating. Most importantly you have to know who you are and what you are about. Going into administration at such a young age my colleagues would ask me, 'How do you become so successful?'. I would answer by saying you must know who you are and like yourself. But knowing who you are and liking yourself is also understanding that you have an Achilles heel, you have limitations. That is what a proactive individual is. A person who is growing and developing; a risk taker. The reactive individual is not the front runner and never will be. Our challenge is to move people who are reactive into a proactive mode.

Dubin: It is generally thought that one of the important traits that leadership has is the understanding of information sources at a school site. What are the most important information sources and how does one get access to that information, and, ultimately, how is that information utilized? How is technology a part of that information source and how is it utilized in the instructional program and as an information source?

Cortines: I think that the most important information source for the principal within a school community are the members of the school community. A principal who does not talk and listen to students intently and know what they are doing and what they are about, and I mean all segments of the school, the academic, sports, co-curricular, fine arts etc., really does not have his/her hand on the pulse of the school. There were several reasons I used to visit classrooms, 1) To understand what was going on. Was instruction really happening? And, 2) To learn myself. To sit and listen to a social science lecture, for example, or to the discussion on a particular phase of literature in an English class; to watch the hands of a student under the guiding eyes of a teacher around a clay pot; to listen to the student council as they were interacting on a particular issue, engaging the faculty in such a way that it provided them the opportunity to be involved, and participate whether or not they agreed with administrator or principal or not. One has to reach out to the community, both on the parents' turf as well as at school and listen to what they have to say. It is essential for a principal to understand the human dynamics within a school community and he can only do this by reaching out to feel the pulse of the school, not just once or quarterly, but every day.

Another important development regarding information systems available to the principal are the assorted new technologies. I respect computers and data processing and what they can instantly do, but I also need to understand how they are viewed by students, staff and the parent community. I respect interactive video, but how would it affect students and especially how would it change a teacher's methodology and his/her means of acquiring new information. How students would respond to this is extremely important. I respect an old fashioned one — the movie — that we show in the classroom which is a type of early technology. But most people did not use it well. We used it as a spacer to take up time rather than as a part of the instructional program. We should have been more attentive to how it would motivate students to engage them in a writing or speaking program. I think also from the standpoint of what goes on in our science labs that we are not doing well with our students unless we provide the state-of-the-art technologies and resultant methodologies which allow students to explore, discover and create, as well as make mistakes.

Dubin: What about information the principal is unaware of?

Cortines: A principal has to be knowledgeable of all of that, but when one is not as knowledgeable as one would like to be, the principal must not be afraid to ask questions, to let students, teachers and parents know that they don't know. Whether you work in a community that has a great number of professional parents, for example, or whether you come from a community that is rural and host to a whole set of technologies foreign to the inner city for example, you have to be willing to let the communities know what it is you know and not know and why it is you want and need to have more information. This can send a very strong message regarding your leadership style as a principal. I believe that some of our new principals do that better than some of us old salts. They haven't been tainted by the rebuffs like, 'Why let it all hang out? You have to be smarter than the community you're supposed to be taking care of'. No, I think that the whole importance of information has to do with the way in which the principal constantly uses information to grow, to develop his/her own skills, whether it is five or ten years before they move on, or whether it is twenty years, or for a lifetime they must be constantly growing, stretching themselves. We have to know what is happening around us and to us. I often ask people, 'How many books have you read? When was the last time you took the time to smell the flowers?'. That is also an information gathering device that has an impact on what you do as a principal and how you motivate and model for students, parents and for teachers.

Dubin: There have been many comparisons that have been made between a CEO of a corporation and the principal at the site level. Are there any distinctions you can draw, comparisons you can make?

Cortines: I think we as educators make a major mistake as we move through the ranks thinking that it changes dramatically at each different level. As a superintendent of three major school districts in California I have noticed that the experiences I have daily do not differ that much from when I was principal or a classroom teacher for that matter. As a teacher of my first sixth grade class of forty two students I was the CEO of that classroom. It was my job to maximize the potential of all forty two students. I was not interested in having them on the same page at the same time in the same reading book. I wanted all forty two balls to be in the air at the same time in whatever area we were exploring, moving at their particular pace. That is difficult. I wanted learning experiences that were good for the entire class and to instill discipline in those who were not as turned on by the learning experience as their fellow student were. The classroom principal, the teacher and the CEO — their goal is to make it work. So I would say there are far more similarities than differences. What makes the difference is our own ego trips, getting caught up in how important we are as we change from level to level, position to position. The sensitivity and understanding of the importance of people is something I learned as a classroom teacher. I also learned that when there was a problem as a classroom teacher I had to deal with it promptly and not sweep it under the rug. Once, for instance, I had a very bright young child in my sixth grade class who always had to have his desk top up. One day I came over to him and in the heat of the moment, I inadvertently slammed the desk top down and yelled, 'Get to work', but accidentally caught his fingers and smashed them. I did get his attention, but I needed to call his parent and let them know that I had done something wrong. I was motivated for the right reason, but I needed to not take the story home, or sweep it under the rug. I needed to let the parent know what happened. That is a situation that I deal with every day as the superintendent, and something I dealt with every day as the principal. There are things that are unpleasant, yet I needed to be pro-active rather than reactive. So I would suggest to you that the issue of leadership really does not change from level to level, position to position. I was fired from my first superintendency and it rattled my confidence a bit in my leadership ability — I had begun to question whether I had what it takes. I was subsequently hired by a city and in a short time became the assistant city manager. I found that the same skills, the same knowledge about myself, the same proactive management style — all of that was just as important. Only the body of knowledge that I was managing had changed. A classroom teacher is a manager, a principal is a manager, and a superintendent is a manager. All three of them are managers of education, instruction and curriculum. While the scoop may change I don't think that much else changes. It is just the numbers and complexities that you have to deal with. I am not so sure that the complexity of a classroom is any different from a school. A classroom teacher can never leave that group of kids. As a principal I could shut the door, or as a superintendent I could avoid certain obligations. It is very important for the classroom teacher to look upon the kinds of experiences he/she has, because how well they deal with issues that come up can easily relate to higher level management issues.

Dubin: In the wave of educational reform there have been many suggestions about the training process for administrators. In fact, in some states there is the idea of not necessarily having a teaching background for effective leadership in schools. What are your thoughts regarding the type of background potential leaders to need have, in order to assume the positions?

Cortines: I think that to be a good or outstanding principal one needs to have very fine liberal arts training. If one does not understand the culture of the society, its art, literature, geography, and history, one is going to have a hard time setting goals with teachers for students and a school community. Also, one has to constantly be engaged in the learning process. That is difficult, because the preparation for the principalship starts in your own school and training. The type of principal you are will be reflective of your own schooling and your own parents' involvement as your natural teachers. The natural teachers' involvement and the professional teachers' involvement when you are very young are contributing factors to the type of principal you will be ... if you have an inquiring mind, for example. To analyze as an adult what is it I didn't have as a young person or in my college training and compensate for that is an ongoing educational process. I feel strongly that teaching experience is important in being a good principal. I am not saying that one could not be a principal having not been a teacher. But I would say that if one was not willing to take the classroom periodically and model what one expected because they have never been a teacher, then they would generally not be a successful principal. A principal is just a master teacher. You need to be able to model and offer suggestions on classroom control, how to encourage discussion in class as opposed to reprimanding the kids or asking them to regurgitate information. If you are going to help teachers look at how they approach thinking skills, you are going to have to be able to give examples, to model and suggest. You may not have been that kind of teacher, but certainly you need to understand what is or is not happening based on the literature. One also needs to have an historical understanding of the various periods of time we have been through. You must have a sense of background ... when, for instance, it was very free flowing and there was really no accountability in teaching; when knowing the multiplication tables was all you needed to know, rather than the ability to put it all together. Yes, you need to know, as Hirsch would say, you need to memorize, you need to know the facts. But, you need to be able to think about those facts and create solutions. Classroom teaching is imperative to this. And as I stated, we need to be careful about moving through the levels syndrome. Some of the most damage we do to aspiring administrators is say that if you want to be a principal you have to be a counselor, then a dean, then department head, assistant principal and, finally, principal. What we do wrong in those situations is never identify the importance of each position; that they could become an end in themselves. For a period of time a counselor may be the most important person in a child's life. A dean that deals with discipline in a compassionate and sensitive manner may save a kid. A department head may provide the direction for a department that is really challenging and helps them look at its curriculum and what they are doing in refreshing and innovative ways. An assistant principal that coordinates all of that is very important.

Dubin: Was that the career path you followed?

Cortines: It is interesting that I was never any of those before I was a principal. My career took me from teacher to an administrative position to the director of long range planning and assistant superintendent and back to the principalship. People thought I was going to fall on my face. What put me in good stead was what I had learned as a teacher. How do you manage? How do you provide control? How do you create? How do you bring kids with different personalities and complexities along? What we need to think about also is not just a professional training. What are your experiences — with a family or without a family? Your experiences on holiday and throughout your life come to bear on what you do as the principal and how you exert leadership. Somebody recently asked me why I opened the schools on Thursday following the earthquake.[1] What were you trying to do, make money off those kids with a higher average daily attendance? I said it has nothing to do with average daily attendance. This is an emergency time. We are going to receive the average daily attendance anyway. I understood the effect that 63,000 kids would have being on the streets of San Francisco. There was the possibility that they would get in trouble. I also realized that another 18,000 would likely not have a good breakfast or lunch and that another 4400 would be on reduced lunch. I also realized that yes, they could sit there and be babysat by a TV and see the earthquake tragedy hour after hour. I also realized that the teacher is probably the most important person within a kid's life other than the parent, and in many urban settings the most important. Therefore, I opened the schools not to make another buck, nor because I believed that every kid should be in school, but I believed it should be available as an option. Was that something I learned in a book? No, after thirty one years being in an educational system and using all of the experiences I had, both good and bad, to hone my ability to make, what I hope to be, the right decision at the right time.

Dubin: What would you consider the most pressing problems facing principals today in our urban settings and how can the information sources you identified earlier help to correct some of these problems?

Cortines: The most pressing problem a principal faces is the ability to stay current considering the rapid speed with which our society is changing, whether it be in the rural, suburban or urban sectors. An awareness that we are educating for the student's world, not ours, is crucial. In my lifetime, technology has been an evolutionary process. In the present student's lifetime, and as a contributing citizen when they become an adult, it is a way of life. We need to make sure that teachers understand that fact and are current. That means exploring and taking risks and introducing in the school some things that may be referred to as 'fads'. It may be finding out what we should not do, rather than just keeping the status quo and playing it safe and being too responsive. The whole current issue is an ability to adapt to the teenagers themselves, to deal with the health issues they are facing, for example. Being current with the issue of substance abuse — drugs — and the issue of AIDS in the urban areas. How do you weave the threads of health education through social science, mathematics, science, physical education and not just relegate it to forty minutes in health class? It is hard to encourage some teachers to stay current because so many say, 'I have only three years to go until retirement', or 'I'm just the new principal', or 'That's someone else's responsibility'. Principals should say every day, as an act of faith, I march to my own drummer. That does not mean you don't work in an in-depth way with the people around you. It means you challenge yourself to be on the cutting edge. That doesn't mean you need to know how to use the computer, or know all the developments in science, but you need to be aware of and accept them. You need to be constantly skimming eighteen periodicals, five newspapers, and the major literary works of the time so as to know what is happening and apply all this to what you are responsible for: the managing of a school.

Dubin: If you could project the role of the principal as well as the role of schools for our greater society in the next five and ten years, how would you see the role of the principal and/or our schools changing?

Cortines: There has to be change in the role of the principal. Because times are changing so fast it is impossible to predict the exact nature of the change. I think the individual has to be able to adapt to situations almost instantly. Whether it is an act of God, such as an earthquake or flood, economic recession, work stoppage, or a student crisis such as a suicide, the principal has to be adaptable. Also, they have to make a connection with an institution of higher learning that is involved with teacher training. It is irrelevant whether it is a rural, suburban, or urban school. There has to be that linkage. They have to find a way that they and their teachers are directly involved with teaching and administrative training. As well, they should attempt to make their institution a lab for training. It would be beneficial for both the institutions that are training teachers and administrators and the schools themselves. If nothing more, it helps them stay current and raises the level of vocabulary from the antiquated to the contemporary. Another changing role of the principal deals with economics. They have to recognize the importance of economics in society. Young people and teachers need to understand that the tearing down of the wall dividing East and West Berlin, irrespective of the symbolic importance, will have a major economic impact. An oil crisis in the Middle East or political unrest in the Philippines or El Salvador will have economic repercussions that may directly affect their lives. That student who will, hopefully, become a contributing citizen needs to understand how and why that is. What we do wrong with kids, especially in high school, is give them the impression that when they leave high school they become 'adults'. Certainly if we look at history over the last several centuries children have had to assume adult roles at a very young age due to various societal problems, e.g., wars, famine, etc. I would submit that the transition to adulthood, responsible citizenship, is a process that begins from birth. The principal, then, whether at the elementary, middle or senior high school level, must be a catalyst in that process ... a catalyst not only with the students, but with the staff as well. Your question asked about what the changing role of the principal would be — well, although this is what he/she should be aware of today, there will be greater demands tomorrow. How do you relate American literature to what is happening at the present time? How do you relate the pains and tragedies in our history or the French Revolution with what is happening today? It is important because it will allow us not only an understanding of the current global condition, but may also help us foresee what may happen ten or fifteen years from now. Adaptability. People sometimes wonder why there seems to be a tendency for the coach or athletic director to be promoted to principal. Every year the coach has a new challenge — a new season, personnel, etc. Every year he/she must adapt to the new circumstances. These qualities of leadership and adaptability that a coach brings with him to a principalship are important, but they alone are not sufficient. Academic excellence and scholarship are also important, but again they are not sufficient in themselves. I remember a case involving the appointment of a principal. He was initially hired as the department chairman. He was the best department chairman we had ever had in a high school. He had a PhD in his field. He had written several books; a true scholar. He was a bummer as a principal. It was because he had not pulled all the other things together.

Dubin: How would you define the principal as you see him/her?

Cortines: The principal is all things to all people. He is a counselor to kids and middle-aged teachers who are undergoing a crisis at home, or to the parent community which may be having economic problems. He is a counselor, a benevolent dictator, a manager, a manipulator, an enforcer, a motivator. He is, in short, adaptable. Paradoxically, let me say that school should not be his entire life; it should not consume him. If it does he will not be sufficiently informed about the world in which he lives. To answer your question then, in the next five, ten or twenty years the principal will have greater pressure to assume the role as a change agent and committed to flexibility and adaptability. I have seen 'change agents' who brought about change, but never changed themselves. It is not good enough to say I know who I am and don't try to change me. Rather, I know who I am and I am evolving as a person. Hopefully, the person does grow and they learn from situations and mistakes and handle them differently and not repeat them. Finally, I believe the principal in the future will have to call on more people for help. He will not be able to do it alone. He will have to look into the school community and include them. People often comment that schools are the least changed institution of the last forty years and that is the problem with them. This can be interpreted as stability. There is more stability in the schools than in those other institutions. In fact, I am not so sure we have done such a bad job. I am suggesting that they need to know when, and how to change, but also what to keep the same. You don't want to throw out the baby with the bathwater. I remember the days of flexible scheduling. At the time that was the panacea. Everyone felt that everybody should be on a flexible schedule. And then there were the days of independent study. If only everyone could just be doing their own thing. There is some good in flexible scheduling and independent study, but it is not the end-all. It is knowing how to take some of the educational fads that come along and *adapt* them to one's own management style and the needs of a particular school. A principal should not *adopt* it as an end-all panacea. Adaptability will be the driving characteristic of tomorrow's principal, coupled with the recognition that the strength of the outside community is an integral part of the educational process.

Dubin: Will the use of data processing, computerized information or other types of information sources impact your schools in the future and change the ways in which they are run?

Cortines: Yes, I do see them impacting. But, again, I would go back to the point that they not become an end unto themselves. They should assist us in managing better, in addressing the needs of students, staff and the school community, in understanding what the patient needs, that they allow us to use more specificity in prescribing the educational process for students and helping staff adapt better. We need to use the information for the good of the student and the school community rather than allowing the various 'programs' and the 'process' dictate and determine our actions. People are often so caught up in the 'process' and the 'program' that they have lost track of its original purpose. I think that being on the cutting edge of information, understanding ourselves and being adaptable are the critical leadership traits required to meet the needs of a complex society.

Note

1   Cortines is referring to the decision he made following the October 1989 earthquake.

Key Points

1   Leadership is developed through years of experience and a willingness to 'take risks'. The leader must be adaptable and able to accept change.
2   Use of technology and information sources is critically important to effective leadership. Ultimately, though, the information sources should be applied so that focus on the interaction among different constituent groups, understanding and being sensitive to their needs is paramount.
3   While the principal must be 'all things to all people', meeting the needs of so many school groups, he must never lose sight of who he is.
4   A proactive decision maker is well-versed in a number of fields and has a greater sense of the world outside his school.

Discussion Questions

1 As a proactive principal concerned with a school site, district, university and business collaboration, what process does Superintendent Cortines suggest be undertaken to develop such a consortium?
2 Is the principal's role in public schools defined differently by the chief executive officers in this chapter? How does Cortines define the role?
3 How does Cortines merge the teacher role into the administrative role?
4 What does Superintendent Cortines mean when he speaks of the principal as a 'risk-taker'?
5 How does Cortines define technology and what application does he envision for it in the future?

Section Three: Jerry Hume: A Corporate Chief Executive Officer's View of a Principal as Chief Executive Officer

William J. Hume, Chairman and CEO of Basic American Foods Corp., was a member of the California Business Roundtable's Education Task Force and has been an active and concerned member of the business community regarding the reform movement in education in the United States. The following interview is a candid acccount of his perspectives on education. He makes specific recommendations regarding student motivation, parental empowerment and teacher recognition within the context of restructuring public education.

Dr. Dubin: What is the principal's role in the wave of educational reform?
Chairman Hume: Everything that I have read about successful schools indicates that it starts with a principal with a vision who articulates that vision to his staff, students, the parents and community and carries out that vision. He is a leader and successful schools begin with a leader with a vision. Leaders must know where they are going. Successful principals know where they are going. It may be demanding excellence from the students, but they have a vision and their schools are characterized by everyone knowing what that vision is and working in the same direction.
Dubin: Would you say that the role of the principal is different today from five years ago and could it be different five years from now?
Hume: I think the role of the principal is the same today as it was five years ago. He is still a leader. The outside world may have changed, but the role of the principal is the same. He is the person to lead the school and articulate that vision. And that will always be the case. Principals need to be able to understand the world about them, what's coming at them in terms of students, parents and society and deal with it. But,

they're still the leaders of the school. No, the principal's role has not changed.

Dubin: If the principal's role remains the same, perhaps the environment has changed. In what ways would you say the environment has changed?

Hume: The environment has changed in a whole series of ways. Let's look at the 1940s. You had a different classroom composition. You had less legal requirements, a less litigious society. You had the ability to discipline students. Now the demands on graduating students in terms of needing higher order thinking skills and lifetime learning are significantly different than the demands for the high school graduate thirty years ago. And, yet, the schools are using the same technology now that they used thirty to forty years ago. The schools have not kept pace with the changing demographics nor have they been responsive to societal problems that have confronted them. Until the schools start improving the education of the students that are in their charge, they are going to fail. Schools have to change in order to deal with the changes society has brought. New advances in learning, for example, cooperative learning as one new methodology, are vehicles which have been developed since the 1940s. Yet, classrooms are still taught in the same ways that they were taught in the 1940s and they are failing grossly. If you have a multiracial classroom as is common today, you don't teach them the same way as you would a homogeneous classroom common forty years ago. Education has to change and it has not. Until it changes it will fail the students and, consequently, the United States.

Dubin: How has this failure and this problem impacted private industry?

Hume: I can quote you some statistics of what business finds is coming out of our schools. Let me give you a series of examples. Chemical Bank of New York must interview forty applicants to find one who can be successfully trained as a teller. What happens to the other thirty nine? IBM found that it had to teach high school algebra to thousands of workers before they could run newly installed computers. And yet Toshiba does not have to train Japanese employees to run computers. They come out of the schools computer literate. Toshiba can then spend money on research and development which, in turn, makes new products, while IBM has to spend the same money on training. Between July and December 1987, 84 per cent of the applicants for entry level positions at New York telephone failed entry level examinations. At Pacific Bell similar entry level tests are required. It recently advertised for entry level non-management jobs in Los Angeles. 258 applicants responded, all of whom were scheduled for testing. 140 of the 258 showed up to take the test. One in fourteen, 7 per cent, of the 140 applicants tested were able to pass the test. Why were 93 per cent of the applicants unable to pass the test? Why did only 54 per cent of the applicants show up for the test? Because they did not have the basic skills or work habits jobs currently available require. You should get those basic skills and work habits in schools but now they are failing the worker.

Dubin: Let's talk about success in schools. What is it about the schools that you have seen as models that have demonstrated the leadership and proactive thinking that makes for a successful, productive student upon graduation?

Hume: Fundamental to a successful school is parent, teacher, student and administration interaction. They are all a part of an integrated whole working in the same direction. The succcessful schools with which I have been involved which include parent, teacher, administration, student and community, have developed master plans which have articulated where they wanted the school to go. Those master plans have embodied the desires of the whole school community. Once the master plan was articulated, everybody knew where they were going and why. There was no misunderstanding about the school's goals and objectives. So, first, you must have a vision for your school, then, once you have articulated the vision you must step aside and let the headmaster or the principal be responsible for carrying out that vision. If the governing body of the school does not like the way the headmaster is implementing the collective vision of the school community, you fire him/her in lieu of another. You don't get involved in what the headmaster does on a day-to-day basis. You hire him to implement your vision and then get out of his way. It is not advisable to reach down into the system and micro-manage what is happening on a day-to-day basis. The principal has to be responsible for running the school, hiring and firing faculty, etc.

Another change I see as important is to review faculty on an annual basis. This would include student critiques for the upper levels in high school and department heads reviewing the performance of the faculty against standards that the school holds for itself. The schools will, thus, not only be driven by a vision, but by standards that it believes are important. The standards are determined by measuring at every grade level the skills and knowledge of each student.

Dubin: Usually there is a conflict between state mandated expectancies in the form of competencies as opposed to the site-level abilities of kids. Sometimes it is hard to bring those kids at the site-level to the expectations of the state level. Is that something that can be reconciled and if so how?

Hume: Absolutely. It is reconciled by taking a look at the way in which we run our schools. We run our schools by the antiquated agrarian model. We still give our children three months vacation during the summer. A child who is failing in school should not be given a three month vacation. He should receive remediatory assistance. We should start to remediate kids as soon as we detect that they are not making the grade. That means as early as kindergarten and certainly by the first and second grades we should administer entrance and exit tests. If the child is not doing well when they come out of kindergarten we should figure out what areas they need help in and remediate and get them up to speed before they go into the first grade. Absolutely, it's possible, we just have to use our time more efficiently. For our schools to shut down when they are failing the nation is a criminal act in my estimation. It's just crazy for that to happen.

Dubin: So early intervention?

Hume: Early intervention, sure. Early intervention with respect to standards. What we want to do is make that child succeed. The last thing we want to do is place that child in a slow learning class. What we really want to do is place that child in the fast learning class and having everyone at the same level. We should look also at ways in which kids can become active in their own learning process as well as that of their peers. That means kids teaching kids. We should not ask our teachers to be solely responsible for the education of our children. How can we get the children involved in teaching each other? I think it is time we recognize that kids sometimes learn a lot better from other kids than they do from their teachers. Do teachers recognize that need? Unfortunately, in most cases, no. They are afraid of losing their authority in the classroom if we turn over some of the responsibility to the kids. It is unfortunate that this and other new learning technologies are met with such resistance from established teachers.

Dubin: With respect to teachers, and let's pursue that for a moment, in the literature and the reform movement there is much talk about professional and career ladders, different types of levels of teacher performance that would constitute different salary levels and so on. Could you speak to that for a moment and, also, how does incentive pay, if it works in the corporate world, affect production, input, involvement and so on?

Hume: I think that the educational establishment has to be evaluated by what it is producing. Teachers have to be measured with respect to whether or not the kids that come out of their class have obtained the skills and knowledge they need in order to be successful at the next level. So, what I would propose is that at every grade level there be a pass/fail exit test. If the child passes they proceed to the next grade. If not, they receive remediation. In addition, the results of the tests are a part of the teachers' performance record. Over a period of time we will be able to identify those teachers and methods which are successful and those that are not. We would be able, then, to help those teachers who lacked the necessary skills do a better job, and, as a result, reduce the number of children they fail. One of the first things we must do is set up standards for each grade level and determine whether the children emerging from each level are meeting the standards. If they are not we must be able to take action to change it. One of the things we must do is to check the current policy of allowing our unsuccessful teachers to remain at their posts year after year.

As for merit pay I think it is important to have a national certification system. There should be an optional test given on a national basis. It would test two things: the skills and knowledge of the teacher, and the teacher's performance. Those teachers who demonstrated the competencies and classroom skills necessary to be successful would be awarded a national certificate. That national certificate would offer tax forgiveness for teachers' salaries over a five year period. Now that is the bonus that I feel is appropriate for those wonderful teachers who have the knowledge, skills and capabilities to be able to win, i.e., be effective in the classroom. I think it should be a national objective to award, recognize, praise, cheer, salute and celebrate those teachers and place them on the pedestal. That is where they should be. On the other hand, those teachers that are failing must themselves be remediated. And if they continue to fail, be removed from the system. So, yes, I do favor merit pay, but in a different way, one that allows teachers national recognition and the respect that they deserve.

Dubin: Is there a similar process in the corporate world with merit pay and incentives?

Hume: Sure. Every time you have a successful employee you want them to help you do your job better. So you promote that winner and recognize them by giving them more and more responsibility. By this public demonstration of approval everyone knows they are a winner. Losers don't stay around long, because you cannot afford them. In business we are driven by having to meet the bottom line. We are not receptive of the public largess on an annual basis. We are responsible to the consumer. If the consumer likes our product and buys it we stay in business. If the consumer does not like our product we change or go out of business. We are consumer driven which means we are accountable to the consumer. We have to make sure our products satisfy a consumer need. Business, thus, lives by consumer choice and accountability. Those are the key criteria that are important for our schools to live by as well. In fact, parents should have the option to choose what school they want their child to attend. Schools should be judged in how well they perform by state, national and international standards. How well do we do against the Japanese, for example? There is a lot of literature that indicates we are not doing very well. The number of scientific graduates we have, versus Japan, or the number of patents we are generating is not promising. Japan is doing quite well right now and we are falling behind. That is unfortunate for our future and the future of our kids.

Dubin: You have alluded to choice as an aspect of parents' involvement. Could you speak to that and how that would work in your opinion?

Hume: The most promising approaches to school reform are those that promote competition between schools and parent choice among schools. There has to be a mechanism in the educational system that informs a particular school as to how well it is doing. This information must be

known before it is documented in a multitude of reports. Parents selecting the school of their choice is a mechanism that indicates to that school
whether or not it is successful. According to the latest Gallup poll, the
majority of American parents want choice. As Checker Finn said, 'Choice
is the reassertion of civilian control over the educational system'. Choice
empowers and motivates. It creates involvement on the part of the
parents which is so necessary for schools to succeed. Choice empowers
those most in need, those adversely affected by the current system; the
poor and minority students who are most apt to be trapped in wretched
schools because their families are unable to afford to move to areas where
better education would be available. Choice is an expression of society's
commitment to equal educational opportunity for all. What is choice?
Public school choice must amount to an open market in which the
consumers are subsidized and the producers are not.

Dubin: Since minority parents have traditionally been uninformed about
the appropriate educational setting for their children, how do they get
informed so that choice for them has meaning?

Hume: We must begin with standards. Standards drive choice. Choice
works best when there is accountability. For example, Al Shanker
reflected the reality of the situation when he said, 'Either you will be
following somebody else's orders, or you are going to have a school that
is run professionally, but with accountability'. Why accountability?
Accountability lets the parents know what they are choosing. Accountability will be the vehicle that will drive intelligent choice. Accountability
reports on the performance of the schools and teachers in accomplishing
what their profession is hired to do: educate the youth. Accountability
is an essential ingredient in motivating people to become performance
driven. Accountability is measuring student accomplishment against the
standard and holding schools accountable for attaining that standard.
Educational accountability is, then, for the individual child and the society at large. Determination that a child attained the necessary knowledge
and learned the skills at one grade level in order to be successful at the
next grade level. How the child did with respect to the standards has to
be communicated to the parents and the teacher. The school's grade level
results must be made available to the press, legislature and the public, so
school performance can be quantified. In this way successful schools can
be recognized, cheered, rewarded, respected and replicated while unsuccessful schools can be identified and motivated to change. Choice will
come through knowledge. Knowledge comes through schools being held
accountable for performance with respect to standards.

Dubin: So that the publicity and the available information about the
success of the school would be communicated to parents, and that would
then allow them to make an appropriate, well thought out decision
about which schools to send their children to?

Hume: Let me give you my vision of that. When the child arrives at school on the first day on his desk will be a notice to take home to his parents which lists what schools he is eligible to go to. In addition there will be information regarding procedures for changing schools, the questions they should ask when searching for different schools, fundamental information about different schools' performance, where they should go to obtain help in changing schools and if they need language assistance where they may receive it. In other words, as soon as a child comes to school they and their parents will be made aware that this school will only hold that child as long as they wish to remain there. That child can, if they wish, go to another school and here is the format and procedures for changing schools if they wish to exercise that choice.

Dubin: So this, in turn, will put the pressure on the schools to make them more sensitive to the market demands?

Hume: You bet, and that happens as soon as the kid gets to school and is provided by the school itself. Different schools would be soliciting different children, because it is in their interest to do that. The system, thus, forces the educational establishment to be responsible to the consumer.

Dubin: Let's refocus on the role of the principal. With respect to leadership in a school and the principal being a proactive decision maker, what methods do you think he can use in order to involve faculty and staff?

Hume: First and foremost, and this goes against the grain of conventional thought, the headmaster has to be responsible for the selection and discharge of faculty. They have to be looked upon as having power so that they can move the school towards the vision implemented by the entire school community. They cannot be forced to take nor keep faculty they don't want. They should be empowered with the ability to hire and fire. Until headmasters have that authority they will be nothing more than figureheads with no real responsibility and no real power.

Dubin: That speaks to the whole issue of empowerment. What I heard you saying is that site-based management really is defined by the principal and the school community, having control of its curriculum, its budget and its hiring?

Hume: Let me refine that a bit. The community, that is the parents communicate to the headmaster or principal the school's vision, and the principal then is responsible for carrying it out. But the community does not impact on the school at all except through the vehicle of the principal. You have to separate the community out from the day-to-day happenings in the school. The principal has to be responsible for that. That is the only way they will be able to craft the school in their own vision. If the community does not like what the principal is doing then they fire them. The school community must have confidence in whom they select and let him run the show. If the community is always watching over the principal's shoulder then all you have is an order receiver not an order giver. You want somebody to be able to use their creativity to carry out the collective vision.

Dubin: The distinction, then, is between policy and vision as opposed to operation?

Hume: Yes. That is what happens in business. Top management in business is responsible for creating the vision, articulating it down into the organization and then getting out of the way. Top management cannot do the day-to-day work. It can articulate, focus and encourage, but the day-to-day work has to be taken care of by the organization. So top management is primarily responsible for looking at where you want to be in the future, articulating that, getting everybody to agree, and helping the organization create that vision.

Dubin: With regard to a better understanding of 'vision', do you think it is necessary for an effective principal to have been a teacher first?

Hume: It certainly makes it a lot easier. I look at my career in business, for instance, having worked many different jobs. I understand the life of the warehouse supervisor, the field manager/buyer, the R&D technician, and the salesman. You have empathy for those people. You understand what they are going through. You celebrate their triumphs and understand their failures because you have been there. So it is important for a principal or headmaster to have had classroom experience.

Dubin: In private enterprise how is technology being used in the form of information sources to make that organization more effective and how can it be used in schools to make them a more effective organization?

Hume: As I look at the work force in the future, people will need to have skills which are different from the blue collar skills in the past. The work force will need to have higher order thinking skills, the ability to draw conclusions from uncertain data, the ability to work in groups, and certainly the ability to work with computers. In the conventional business office, for example, word processors have replaced typewriters. In this office nobody uses a typewriter anymore except for very unusual tasks that don't work with a word processor. Everything is done with word processors and laser printers. You have to be able to not only use but enjoy the extension of the capabilities that the computer and its software give you. I and the people I work with are able, for instance, to do things which, if we had to do it with a pencil and paper and calculator, would require so much more time. Right now we are technologically driven just in the office place, let alone in the workplace. Look at a processing line, for example. It is characterized now by very few people. It is almost 100 per cent automated nowadays. You have people responsible for running the computers that run the line. Very little manual work is done. It is higher order work. You have to be able to program computers, understand processes and equipment, and be able to change them from a central information source. So being a successful employee now means having the skills to interface with the equipment and technology that are necessary for business to be able to compete. Increasingly sophisticated technologies are in the workplace and our employees need to use, be comfortable with and improve on those technologies. One of the things we have been able to do is improve our efficiency dramatically. We have taken an idea out of the universities or literature, worked on it and improved it. You have to get comfortable with the idea that there is no one solution to a problem but a number of solutions. You have to be able to be comfortable with continuous change. Above everything else change most characterizes the modern workplace. If we were producing things today the same way as ten years ago we would be absolutely uncompetitive and out of business. That is how much we have changed.

Dubin: As far as schools are concerned, how do you think they need to utilize technology?

Hume: I don't think technologies or the lack thereof in schools is the issue. I'll give you a sense of what the schools should be responsible for. The National Academy of Sciences says that the knowledge and skills needed by students in the future are command of the English language, reasoning and problem solving abilities, reading and writing skills, computational skills, knowledge of and the ability to apply the scientific method, oral communication skills, interpersonal skills, knowledge of our history, society and economic system, positive work habits and attitudes. Those are what our citizenry in the future have to have under their belt. That is what the schools have to feel they are responsible for in teaching our children.

Dubin: Is there a way in which the effective leader anticipates the change you have identified? And what would you say the distinction is between a proactive decision maker and a reactive one? If you could also speak to the difference in what you have seen in the corporate as well as the educational world.

Hume: In life you basically want to take charge of your future. I have a saying, you can change the future but you can't change the past. I believe we in the United States can change our future. We can let it be the way it is. We can allow 700,000 functional illiterates emerge out of our schools every year and have a nation go from a first, to second to third rank status. That is a result of accepting the status quo. We can say, however, that the status quo is unacceptable and we are going to do something about it. That means changing the way things are done. As I have said previously, two key criteria for the public schools are encouraging parents' involvement and creating standards by which to measure teacher and school performance. Parents, empowered with the ability to choose among schools, will force them to respond. Schools, seeing their enrollment drop will, indeed, respond. We cannot afford to be in a reactive situation as far as the school is concerned, which is what we are doing right now. We are reacting to teenage drop-outs, we are reacting to drugs, we are reacting to teenage pregnancy. We have to be proactive. We have to have a vision of where we want to be. The children want to be successful citizens. They know the vision of Horatio Alger is just as much for them as anyone else. They want to have a part of the American dream. We, the citizens that have benefited from the educational system that has brought the country to this stage, have to take the responsibility for seeing that the schools are brought up to the level where the children that come after us can obtain the same benefits, skills and knowledge and lead the same type of successful lives that we have. Right now the schools are failing miserably because they are not responsible to the consumer. They don't have standards by which they can be judged. Take report cards, for example, the schools' primary mechanism for conveying information to the parent. They are a farce. A report card evaluates that child with respect to the other children in the class. That does not tell you a thing. That child could be reading in the seventh grade at a third grade level, and if they get an 'A' on their report card the parents are happy. But his parents are not being told that their child is failing in terms of not having the skills needed to succeed later on. We have to adopt a different method of reporting. That method will report how well those children are doing versus standards. It is with the criterion of standards that we measure succccess, after which we allow the parents to select the school they want. We become proactive by drafting legislation which changes the rules of the game. It is time to stop pouring more money into and buoying up a failing system. Business must stop squandering its money by spending it on a one–on–one basis in the schools. That is not going to help the school system. Business has to change the rules so that the school system can help itself.

Dubin: I want to follow up on something you alluded to earlier and that is how we are locked into the agrarian timetable. Do you have any ideas about how the timetable would change? Generally the school year is approximately 181 or 186 school days per year.

Hume: Yes! In Japan it is 240. Here in Fairfield, California they have year-round schools. They were brought to year-round schools because they could not afford to build four school buildings but had to settle for three. Why should you not go to year-round schooling? Often times over the summer, the children go backwards.

Dubin: So you would recommend another type of mode, one that demands more school days?

Hume: Yes, one that would not have a mandated summer vacation. One could take vacations any time of the year. What you hear is that parents don't want it. I don't believe that. I believe the football and basketball coaches and the teachers who want their vacation don't want it, but if you ask the parents and explain to them — the parents are as frustrated as heck during summertime. They realize their kids are going to be out not learning for three months in the summertime. They don't know what to do with their kids. Parents basically do want year-round schooling or at least the option. So I think the educational establishment is misleading us when they say there would be a great deal of resistance to year-round schooling. I think they are self-serving in terms of encouraging parents to resist that rather than explain to the parents the benefits. If you have to have air-conditioning than you have to have air-conditioning. It's a heck of a lot cheaper than building a bunch of new school buildings.

Key Points

1 Schools will be held more accountable to public demands for improvement in student performance than ever before.
2 Teachers must be more effective in preparing students for the work force and be compensated appropriately.
3 Not only should principals have the necessary information sources available to them in making decisions, i.e., computer technology, demographics, etc., but the schools should be providing the type of curriculum for our students that reflects the high tech age we live in.
4 The proactive decision maker should be 'empowered', i.e., given the authority to determine the philosophy, direction and use of resources to move and manage his school forward.

Discussion Questions

1 How is parent choice defined by Hume?
2 The areas of school 'report cards' and 'accountability' are defined differently by these CEOs. How are they defined and what does Hume think will result if schools don't 'make the grade'?
3 Inadequate funding is often seen as a perpetual soft spot in public education. 'How are they defined and what does Mr. Hume think will result if schools don't "make the grade?"'
4 What type of reaction would you anticipate from the educational community regarding Hume's remarks about our public schooling? Please explain.
5 When Hume states that students are ill-prepared academically for the job market, he also identifies student deficiencies associated with responsibility and values. How do the two areas interrelate and what expectations does he have of our schools in this regard?
6 What type of creative funding sources does Hume identify as viable for public education?

Section Four: Henrietta Schwartz, Dean, School of Education, San Francisco State University

Dean Schwartz received her BSE from Northern Illinois University in English, Speech and Drama (1950), an MA from Northwestern University in

Anthropology (1962), her MEd from Loyola (1966), and her PhD from the University of Chicago in Educational Administration (1972). Dean Schwartz has numerous publications focusing on administration, leadership, teacher training, organizational change and curriculum in refereed journals throughout the nation. Her research has been in anthropology and she has been active with committee work and professional organizations. She has been a key note speaker at AACTE, AERA and many other national associations and consultant to educational districts throughout the country.

Dr. Dubin: What is the role of the principal in the wave of educational reform?

Dean Schwartz: It is critical, next to the central role of the teacher. In any kind of real reform, that is classroom level reform, the principal has the responsibility and the power, and hopefully, the skills and the knowledge to restructure the context of the school to facilitate what it is the teacher and the student do together which, presumably, is learning. The principal is the facilitator. He ('he' used in the universal sense, meaning a person of either gender) is the vision maker, the symbol manipulator, the resource manager, the values mentor and the keeper of the ethics and standards for that school building. His role is, therefore, critical. Demands on himself and his staff are virtually superhuman given the nature of resource allocation to American public schools. As far as I am concerned a good principal is in the nature of a folk hero. Reform can be done without him in a very haphazard fashion. With the principal's active participation, reform can be done extraordinarily well — efficiently and effectively. I don't think reform can be achieved at the local grassroots level without the principal.

Dubin: What do you think constitutes a proactive decision maker and how would you define a reactive decision maker?

Schwartz: Let me start with the reactive first. There was a paper and later a chapter done by Nancy Pitner that talked about the congruence between graduate training programs and educational administration, and the demands of the workplace at the principals' level. She then pointed out the discrepancies. In graduate training programs a great deal of value is placed on logic and reasoning as well as the written word and reflection. In the real world, the principal is frequently asked to behave emotionally, to make immediate decisions without time for reflection while, for instance, talking to somebody in the corridor. Indeed, most of the things that are accomplished by principals are in face-to-face interaction without carefully constructed written directives or even documentation. A great deal of importance in the graduate program is placed on genuflection to authority. One reviews the literature, uses the theoretical framework that is fashionable at the time, attaches oneself to a guru for writing one's dissertation and, by and large, reflects what this wise person believes, thinks and has done. The real creative doctoral student is able to give it a twist, make some of it his own. But there is very little original research that goes on at the traditional dissertation level. Consider the difference with respect to a decision or a major project which is undertaken by a principal of a school. Citing authority, for many of the teachers in the building, often invokes the bureaucratic bogie man. Frequently, authority is so oppressive that the really creative principal is encouraged by his own values and by his creative peers, to find ways to get around authority, or to ignore it. That which is home grown is valued more by teachers then their slavish adherence to something that is currently in fashion. So that is another discrepancy. One could cite a whole litany of these, but there are two or three more we need to talk about. The point is, most of the preparation programs at the graduate level that certify and train school building administrators, do so with the notion in mind that he is going to be at the cutting edge of reform in his field. So that means that the practitioner has to generate, pretty much for himself, a plan of action, with the assistance of some wise mentors in the field, perhaps people at the university who are teacher oriented. And here the operative word is *plan*.

I think the most critical feature of the principal as a leader is the ability to plan and involve people in the planning process. There are four components to planning: one is generating the vision, to borrow the Peters and Waterman jargon. I prefer to call it establishing a cosmology or value structure; the 'oughts' of behavior and belief for that particular system. It is up to the educational leader to do that and to be very articulate, to make public pronouncements and make sure the language being used is understandable by the participants in that system, and to repeat the message often and in a variety of ways. So one must get people to buy into the value system. That means the administrator has to establish a series of rights and rituals and rewards for people who engage themselves in this cosmology and this value system. That comprises the first part of planning. The second part is to establish a social organization and governance system that will facilitate the plan — a council, a curriculum group, a problem solving task force, or a committee of concerned teachers — and to get that group to focus the agenda so that some reasonably precise goals are established for what that group wants to do. The third part of planning is to work with the group, to generate a working level of trust. By trust I mean, 'I believe you when you say you are going to do "x" in a timely fashion and likewise'. One needs to generate an action plan: what are we going to do and when? And how are we going to monitor this? Then, what the administrator has to do is establish an economic system that gives back to the group the resources it needs to implement its plan. The fourth part of planning is very simple but critical: documentation and monitoring, that is to say, evaluation. This leads to data that help you fine tune the system. It is all very nice and logical, but, given the 2000 crises an administrator faces in the day-to-day operation of the school, how does a principal generate the time to do this? If we were running year-round schools for instance, or if the principals were paid to take a month in the summer and do this kind of thing, reflect upon it, performing a careful analysis of what exactly has transpired in their system, I think we could run much more productive schools. The principal orchestrates this whole thing. He is a conductor, sometimes with a soloist, sometimes with a group of virtuosos and an ensemble, and sometimes with an entire orchestra. He must know the music, the curriculum. He must be sure the players know, understand and can transmit the curriculum. This is essential.

Dubin: Generally what characterizes an effective principal is his ability to identify information sources, to make him proactive as opposed to reactive. What types of information sources need to be identified?

Schwartz: First, he must have a knowledge of the approved curriculum and an overview of the disciplines which undergird the K-12 curriculum. Then, traditional demographic information, of course. Let me preface my remark by making sure that the principal knows the difference between information and gossip. In that respect the principal has to be an on-the-site researcher, seeking for the truth just as an historian or anthropologist does, verifying his sources through procedures of internal and external evidence, through more than one key informant. Hopefully, the standard of research and data collection techniques are part of the principal's repertoire of skills in order to distinguish necessary important information from background static. All school organizations typically have a great deal of noise in their system. I think it is critical that the principal have available a set of skills to distinguish the signal from the noise. The first thing a principal needs in using information has to do with a set of guidelines for verity. The good old stuff like reliability and validity and generalizability. Those processes are just as important when dealing with a living culture, as when dealing with a table of random numbers. What the principal needs is demographic information about the faculty, students and the community. And he needs to be able to manipulate that demographic information so he needs computer skills. He needs to be able to aggregate it and disaggregate it. He needs a comprehensive knowledge of the curriculum and the pocket of excellence. He needs a sense of ceremony, of ritual. For example, if he is the principal of a large secondary school it may be very important for him to know how many single men and women are on the faculty and what the age cohorts are. This information is important in planning social kinds of activities. Do you organize singles' activities or other activities more suited for married couples, i.e., banquets, picnics, dinner dances, or whatever the social events are? The principal should have a knowledge of demographic information such as age, sex, marital status, and race, if available. One might also want to do a personal interest survey of the faculty to find out what their academic and personal interests are. This would transmit to them that you value them as human beings, and you do, and you should. It also gives information about club sponsorship potential. When I was principal in Chicago with a very large faculty of 264 faculty members, by doing that kind of hobby interest survey we were able to establish a fencing club with a sponsor that ultimately took the group to a state championship. Among other things, that supported the academic program. That is what the information is useful for. The same should be true of the student population and there I would talk to my coaches and find out what it is that students think is important. I would even survey the students as well, to find out what they do after school or would like to do after school. Much of this should be discrepancy analysis survey stuff, i.e., what should be, and what is. This gives the principal information about the ways in which your constituents' aspirations and expectations are congruent with those of the teacher and the school.

Dubin: What else would you do?

Schwartz: The second thing I would recommend is to find out what teachers know about students on a class by class, grade level and school basis and compare that with what really is. Do teachers really know who the students are, what they dream about and do after school? Because if you don't that is your first disservice to your school community. The same thing would be true about the community. I would collect all the information that I could and make sure it is updated. Once again, the storage of that information in ways in which it can be manipulated by a computer is critical. That implies that the principal must have such skills. Nothing terribly elaborate, mind you, but certainly some ability to do SPSS if necessary and D-BASE spreadsheets. So, demographic information about the community, students, faculty and support staff. The second set of data bases that a principal needs are those having to do with curriculum and instructional needs fiscal resources and the status of the instructional materials in the building and what's available from special programs, the State, Feds, local service agencies, foundations and so on. In other words, the series of data banks allows the principal to know what the state of his resources is currently and what is available in the broader community that he might be able to tap into. This may be accomplished simply by going to a Lions Club meeting and asking them to help start a tutoring program, or going to a foster grandparents' meeting at the local church or temple and getting them to start a tutoring program, or finding out what sorts of industries may be in the school service area that would care to donate some materials, or money or give a special award to a child. So the principal needs information that is updated and which he or she can manipulate concerning various needs and potential resource bases. The third set of information that he needs, as principals have to be politicians too, is the nature and expectation of his superiors and the board of education and other power brokers in the community. Let's assume once again you are a principal of a high school and you have several athletic events this weekend to concentrate on. Your attendance is desired at both events and you have no particular preference as to which one to attend. You know, however, that the Mayor and the Merchants' and Manufacturers' Club President just love basketball. Maybe that is where you ought to go, because you want scholarships for those kids, or a remodeled chemistry lab., or specimens for the biology classes, or new band uniforms; the LEA is not going to pay for these things. Also, you want visibility and status for your teachers and your school, because all institutions need heroes. That kind of information is important too. This information is collected and kept inside one's own head. As part of that, it is important to know what civic and community events are absolutely critical to attend and to be a visible actor. If the superintendent throws a reception every year around Christmas time and expects to see all the principals there, you better know that, not so much for your own career, but for responses to requests by you or your teachers and students. So it is a question of knowing the territory and making sure you are a principal actor in that scene. Finally, the principal needs to have ongoing formative and evaluative data of the productivity of school programs. That means you build in the evaluation from the get-go ... not to the point that it is oppressive, but you devise ways in which teachers can fill in something monthly where you can verify the data and get some notion as to how the academic programs are going. For example, if one of your goals is, within the next year, to show that the range of the reading scores of all fourth graders is within two months of 4.5, you had better have a quarterly testing program with a data reporting procedure and some way of analyzing it so that you may determine where remediation is needed. So, I think you need performance and outcome measurements with some incentive system that builds in ongoing awards and appropriate sanctions.

Dubin: With respect to the role of the principal today and how you project the principal's role in the future, what would you say will be the significant differences in the ways he or she would manage and make decisions?

Schwartz: Those who don't know their history are doomed to repeat it. You have to look at the history of the evolution of the role of the principal before you can make any predictions. The role of the principal in the United States started with the notion of the headteacher. And in many small school districts, certainly in rural areas, the principal is still a teacher. As the role developed and became specialized and voluntary professional associations sprang up, particularly during the fifties, the principal was in many way the ruler of his castle. Specialized training programs prepared principals. Principals were viewed as professionals in the same way as lawyers and accountants and other people with special expertise who were brought in to do something esoteric, without lay interference. In other words, the principal pretty much determined what went on in the schools. It was very important for individual teachers to behave in ways that were congruent with the principal's wishes, programs and demands. The schools functioned fairly well if you had a knowledgeable, benign despot. They did not function very well if the emperor had no clothes and nobody bothered to tell him. In some ways the fifties and sixties were the heyday of the school administrator because they behaved very much like doctors. They protected their own and even in cases of rampant malpractice, it was rare that you saw a principal fired. But, the trains ran on time, and schools were viewed as doing a reasonably good job in giving us the competitive edge in the world market. Now Sputnik was a bit of a setback, but by the time we landed a man on the moon it was pretty clear that the American schools were still doing what everyone expected them to do. Nobody bothered to check and see how American schools were doing with ethnic minorities, linguistically diverse student populations, poor, disadvantaged, and the so called underprivileged youth. Then Coleman made public the news that schools were not doing very well and the years of decline in respect and status for schools began. The community trust eroded, not just for the principal but for the teachers. New York, ten years ago, and Chicago presently are extreme examples of public distrust and denial of the professional role of the principal and of the teacher. When both researchers and the popular media say that the community knows more about how students shall be educated, how teachers shall be taught, how principals shall administer, than the professional, this is not inclined to make the profession an attractive one for the best and the brightest to want to enter. Those are the extremes because the most dismal failures in American public education have been in urban education. This is not to say that there are not rural schools in trouble in California, Texas, Appalachia and so on. Further, we cannot condemn every school, every principal, every teacher in the nation because of the severe problems in a percentage of schools. For example, Fred Hess's report last year that led to major restructuring of the governance schools in Chicago, indicates that at least a third of the schools in the city at the elementary level are doing quite well. Of the sixty-four Chicago high schools there are twenty of them that are offering exceptionally fine programs. In fact, every secondary school in the city has one or two programs that are extraordinarily efficient and successful with inner city populations. So, what is the lesson to be learned? Well, a couple of things. It says that as a group principals are not learning from each other. They are not sharing the essential features of their successful programs and activities with their colleagues. They are not tapping into the wisdom of their own practice. Maybe one of the things they need to do is to look to the university to help them chronicle and disseminate what it is they do well and under what conditions this is replicable. They need to develop some skills and some guideposts to determine what is so idiosyncratic that it cannot be transferred and is dependent on the excellence of a curriculum, the charisma of a teacher, a principal and/or a wonderful mix of students and teachers. These unique events are typically called the golden years in any system. But what is it that is universal, that with modifications anybody can do? That is the critical question. How do you achieve and sustain a 'wonderful mix'? The answers to this question allow leaders to blend theory and practice in a preparation and ongoing staff development program and in a school. My first hope is that attention to theory, as well as this transference of successful practices, are among the features that will be incorporated into newly configured professional preparation courses and programs — a both/and approach to the training of principals. It seems to me the second thing that needs to and probably will happen in the future is some form of acknowledgement of, for lack of a better word, trait/treatment interaction.

Dubin: How would you define trait/treatment interaction?

Schwartz: What I mean is there are ways of acknowledging the special strengths of an individual and a particular set of needs of a system. Presumably head-hunters specialize in this. At the universities we call it selection models. It seems to me more and more that we have to systematize the way in which we search and select educational leaders so that we don't get a mismatch. Private schools tend to do that pretty well. They are not afraid of turning over leadership if an individual does not fit. Public schools don't pay much attention to that. More importance is placed on seniority, that is, who applies for the position. I really do believe we have to be more systematic about that. So, again, paying close attention to the Chicago model will be very interesting, because there the community has the right to do that. Let's see how sophisticated they get. I am sure there will be more systematic selection and placement of principals in the next decade. I am not so sure about what is going to happen with the series of things that are in fashion right now. It is a little too early to tell what the impact will be of such things as the 'principal as instructional leader', 'the principal as the reflective practitioner', 'the principal as the site-based manager', 'the principal as a symbol maker'. What each of these thrusts in the literature is going to produce in terms of selection, placement and expectations for principals' performance in the twenty-first century has yet to be seen. It would be nice if the principal could be all of those things. However, I am not sure they are all compatible, or if, in fact, having a principal doing all of those things at the same time in the school is not going to make for a very frenetic system with a lack of focus. If we believe in the efficacy of our research, we need to be more scientific and generate some models that the research indicates are pretty apt to work. Once again you can't put a limit on or a fence around individual aspirations. If an individual wishes to be a secondary principal in a large urban district and everything you know about him tells you right away he would really be better off as the principal of an elementary school in a suburban, homogeneous district, there is nothing you can do to stop him from achieving his own career goals. However, if we can just do a couple of real ethnographic and longitudinal case studies that permeate the literature and get into the training programs, ultimately to affect superintendents' thoughts and the ways they evolve their selection mechanisms, we could achieve a more scientific method of matching person to place and a job. If we can do this, then we might have a chance to make dramatic differences in education. Finally, I think principals are going to have to be smarter, better educated and, to borrow a phrase from business, 'bottom-line' directed. The push toward assessment and productivity measures will impact the way in which principals are prepared and how they perform. I would hope that the best and the brightest of the field stay with us and go into the educational roles that are so critical for our nation's future. Also, principals will have to reconnect with the classroom and community leadership. There are a whole set of dilemmas that they are going to have to face, not much different than the dilemmas that have been faced over the last fifty years; do you teach the curriculum or the child? do you emphasize equity vs. excellence, do you focus on standardization vs. individualization? Can one do both/and? For example, do you treat all teachers the same or do you differentiate on merit and on what criteria for merit? I also think the principal is a part of his culture, bringing to the job the values, prejudices, behaviors and knowledge of that culture.

Schools have tremendous cultural ballast. They have looked the same for the last 2000 years since the days of the academy; a learned adult instructing a group of unlearned neophytes in the ways of productive citizenship and adulthood. They way in which you organize the subject matter, the adults, the students and the context are the dependent variables that the principal can manipulate to influence the independent variables of school outcomes. What will schools look like in the twenty-first century; in many ways, much like they look today. In other ways, if we are as intelligent and moral and generous and concerned about people as we say we are, schooling will look very different and will do better things for kids.

Key Points

1 A proactive decision maker is one who involves people in planning, provides an appropriate governance structure in which to operate, creates a high trust condition for healthy interaction among members and an evaluative process for feedback.
2 Identifying, amassing and evaluating information is crucial for proactive decision making.
3 Proactive principals understand their school culture and respond accordingly; they are highly visible at the school and provide

necessary support for their staff and students and are connected to the needs of the community.

4 Principals will be held more and more accountable in the age of educational reform. Schools are under close scrutiny by the greater community and at the same time are being asked to help correct ever increasing problems endemic to our society.

Discussion Questions

1 What does Dean Schwartz allude to when she speaks of the principal as a cultural leader?
2 Dean Schwartz refers to K-12 site-based management as being crucial to effective proactive leadership. Please explain.
3 According to Dean Schwartz, when specific proactive leadership characteristics are identified, they can be quantified and provide the underpinning for administrative training. What position would you take regarding the likely identification of these traits? Do you believe that effective leadership is intuitive or can it be instilled?
4 Can 'cultural' leardership be transmitted by leaders whose backgrounds don't reflect the students' background? How?
5 Dean Schwartz offers a leadership assessment and analysis that is founded in socialization theory. What socialization process is she alluding to in her remarks?

Effective School Processes: Analyses by Professors of Educational Administration

Introduction

Chapter 4 consists of four sections: Proactive Decision Making: Step To College and Mission To College Programs; Administrative Computer Information Systems; Supportive Supervision: Leadership for the Twenty-First Century; and Decision Making Through the Use of Interactive Video. In the section on proactive decision making written by Professors Brizendine and Perea, a comprehensive analysis of a school undergoing a radical change process was conducted. Brizendine and Perea analyzed the program initiatives, interviewed the administrative personnel and reviewed documentation in order to provide 'in the trenches' research material on proactive and reactive decision making and what effective and ineffective processes emerged as the school underwent change.

Professor Jonsson presents a comprehensive review of the computer systems available in the schools and identifies ways in which the information generated can be utilized to make proactive decisions. He addresses areas such as budget, salary, and scheduling as to how information is integrated to better understand the interrelationships of information. This is critically important to effective principals since it allows them to see the entire school process in a holistic manner, interdependent and organic, changing and evolving and not operating in a vacuum.

Professor Rothstein presents a social/psychological perspective that focuses on the role of the effective, proactive principal as he relates to and involves himself with his teacher colleagues. In his section on supportive supervision, he analyzes the psychological forces that underlie the complex motives behind human interaction. This far-ranging insight provides the principal with crucial information about human behavior. This type of information allows the principal to be proactive in decision making, providing appropriate conditions that would allow people to function effectively and with fewer constraints. Professor Rothstein provides several examples which illustrate this dynamic process as well as effective supervisory approaches.

The fourth section within Chapter 4 focuses on interactive video. In this section, I provide the backdrop to cognitive mapping and how that application relates to interactive programming. I also offer a specific case study which outlines the process of utilizing interactive video while analyzing the decision involved in the case study. The decision-making options are identified as well as the consequences triggered by the choices selected.

Section One: Proactive Decision Making: Step To College and Mission To College Programs*
Emily Lowe Brizendine and Jacob E. Perea

Brizendine teaches in the Educational Administration Department at California State University at Hayward. Perea specializes in Bilingual Education and is the Chair of the Department of Administration and Interdisciplinary Studies at San Francisco State University.

Introduction

Attempts to understand and describe the role of the school principal have been central to the development of the knowledge base and preparation programs of school administration. Studies have approached the topic of school leadership from many conceptual perspectives (Ogawa and Bossert, 1989). Underlying these perceptions are various assumptions regarding the authority of the principal, the nature of the relationship between the administration and teachers, the organizational context of the school and conceptualization of how schools function.

The latest in this line of inquiry borrows from the business world the notion of the principal as chief executive officer. There are various factors contributing to this interest. Recent research on school improvement has identified the school as the locus for meaningful change to occur (Goodlad, 1983). In addition, reform efforts focusing on the restructuring of schools or site-based management engender a perception of an increase of autonomy and decision making authority of site principals. Although there is no clear consensus on what is meant by 'restructuring schools', (Olsen, 1988), bureaucratic decentralization is common to most restruc-

* Special appreciation to Lupe Tiernan and Pat Aramendia for their support and contribution in this section.

turing efforts (Timar, 1989). This shift of control and decision making to the school site level contributes to an interest in examining possible changes and alternative models of school leadership and functioning.

A recent report by the National School Board Association (*San Francisco Chronicle*, 1990) reported that school districts are increasingly called upon to provide services that address the problems and concerns of the larger society. In addition to being confronted with problems of student discipline, teacher and administrator shortages and recruitment, they take on responsibility for AIDS education, teenage pregnancy prevention, substance abuse prevention, early childhood education and desegregation.

For the urban school, the impact of societal problems is particularly severe due to the intensity and higher concentration of such problems at one location. In addition, such schools often have a disproportionate number of 'at risk' students whose backgrounds do not prepare them for the kind of education provided through the traditional structure and instructional methods of schools. For the urban school principal, pro-active decision making is a desired goal and practice as means to systematically address specific student needs and to manage the school environment whose boundaries are ever more permeable and increasingly expanding.

This chapter is a case study of the Step-To-College (STC) and Mission-To-College (MTC) programs at San Francisco's Mission High School. It attempts to identify significant factors and the process undergone by this urban comprehensive high school to develop a program to reduce their drop-out rate and increase the number of graduates going onto college. It focuses on the ability of the principal and the administrative team to acquire and identify relevant facts and information related to the school's most pressing problems. In addition, it examines their ability to establish an administrative structure that capitalized on identifying key personnel and the necessary functions which contributed to the creation of a climate of change that supported and guided the evolution of the program. This case study of the development and evolution of the programs is presented here as illustrative of ways in which the principal and her administrative team can be proactive in addressing one of the major chronic problems of urban schools — high drop-out rate of minority students.

As in all analogies and resulting metaphors used to describe the nature of school leadership, the functionality of the analogy is limited by context specific factors. In respect to this case study, discussions regarding the principal as a chief executive officer recognize several limiting factors: first, the degree to which the principal has control over areas of school that impact the day-to-day functioning of the school, that is, budget; second, the impact of federal, state, and district policies and mandates, that is, district teacher affirmative action hiring policies, credentialing and teacher placement, and category of students that can be served by various funded programs; and finally the fact that although a school principal has authority and responsibility for an important unit of schooling, she is at the end of a larger organization that for the most part has operated within a structure that is basically hierarchical in nature.

This case study of Mission High School's programs reflects the constraints and possibilities of preemptive, proactive administrative action within the social, cultural and organizational context of schools. The school did not undergo a restructuring of its student population, its teaching staff or its curriculum as precondition for establishing these programs. These changes often times create a friendly climate for the success of programs aimed at improving student achievement. Rather, the changes that took place at Mission High School occurred in an evolutionary and ecological manner.

The initial Step-To-College program was not a result of a rational process consisting of gathering relevant data, considering all possible alternatives and costs, involving significant participants in the schooling process (parents, students, and teacher), and selecting the best possible solution. Rather, the program came into existence as a result of a chance confluence of several conditions and key individuals from various educational levels with a common interest in improving achievement levels of minority students. Once STC was established, however, the desire to ensure its success led to the need to control the factors affecting its operation, and the need to garner resources and support. These efforts are examples of proactive behaviors. They led to the development of the Mission To College program. Thus, for the decision makers of the school, the programs can be viewed as vehicles for proactive decision making and systematic analysis and planning for addressing school problems.

Background of Programs

Step To College Program

Step To College (STP) is an academic-based program for increasing the numbers of minority students attending four year colleges. The program was developed by a professor at San Francisco State University with the Principal and Vice Principal of a predominantly Hispanic San Francisco public high school, in response to a study conducted by the California State University system that found many African American and Hispanic students who graduated from high school are not prepared to enter four-year institutions (*Hispanic and Higher Education: A CSU Imperative*, 1985, quoted in Perea, 1989). An intent of the program is to take students who are not expected to graduate nor attend college and offer them university courses that will give them skills needed for college success while still in high school so that they can see college attendance as a realistic possibility for them.

Important program components include: recruiting and advising high school students during their junior year in high school; offering these high school students college enrollment in university courses and Freshman status at San Francisco State University during their high school senior year; assisting their transition to the university; and providing support for them when they become full-time students.

The freshmen college courses offered to the high school seniors meet general education requirements and generate university credits which are transferable. Taught by university faculty from academic departments, the courses are held at the high school site after school once a week for three hours. A goal of these courses is to demystify academia. Crucial to the success of this program is the necessary close collaboration between the university and the high school and school district to facilitate procedures for admission to the university. While the initial participants were Hispanic students, the program now includes African Americans, Native Americans, low-income whites and Southeast Asians.

Program successes

In 1984, a year prior to the implementation of Step To College, university enrollment records indicated that only two Mission High School graduates enrolled at San Francisco State University, a nearby four-year institution. According to Mission High School records, no other Hispanic students went on to a four-year institution that year.

The success of the program can be evidenced in retention and performance data of the first graduates of the program who are now juniors and seniors at San Francisco State University. From that initial pilot program at Mission High School during the 1985–86 school year, seventeen Hispanic graduates went on to enroll at San Francisco State University in the fall, 1986. As of 1988–89 school year, eight students have left the University. Their combined grade point average was 2.5. None of the students left the University because of poor grades (Perea, 1989).

Of the remaining students, grade point averages ranged from 2.2 to 3.4 with the median of 2.7. Their undergraduate majors included Nursing, Engineering, Industrial Technology, Business, Computer Science and Psychology. Background data of this group of STC students revealed that they do not fit the traditional college student profile. For example, only two students were native-born; they were recent immigrants with an average of less than four years in the country; the average combined SAT score for the group was 680 points; and only one in the group had decided to attend college prior to participating in STC. In spite of the group's characterization as not being traditional college students, they have remained in college and have demonstrated ability to be successful college students.

Critical program elements
While recruitment programs for underrepresented minorities or granting college credit for university level work done in high school are not new, the STC program has certain critical elements that seemingly contribute significantly to its success. Perea identified several key elements:

STC is presented as a high status, attractive program rather than a remedial, second-best program;

the consistent message communicated to students in the program by high school teachers, administrators and university instructors is that they can succeed in college;

the program has as its major objective the removal of barriers and not the lowering of standards in assisting the students to succeed;

the support given to the students in the program and continued through their transition to the university constitutes an ongoing 'surrogate family' support group that is consistent with and supplements the cultures of the students;

all teachers adapt teaching methods and materials to the cultural and educational backbrounds of students;

STC does not take the 'cream' of the class, rather the program is open to all seniors. (This was identified by the first group of Hispanic students in the program as an important feature. They felt if the program was special then all students should have the opportunity to participate in it.);

the collaborative effort and cooperation that exist between the university and high school is valued and genuine, rather than perfunctory;

key individuals in both the university and high school have the vision and belief that these students can succeed and therefore work to remove all barriers to locate support among colleagues and administrators to make the program possible.

Mission To College Program
Early in the initial years of Step To College, the administrators and teachers in the STC program realized that to ensure its long term success and its ability to indeed provide traditionally non-college-bound students the skills and the required courses to get into that track, the students must be brought into the program earlier in their high school years. As a result, a pilot college core curriculum program named Mission To

College began in the 1987–88 school year involving 150 ninth graders. Significant components of MTC include:

establishing a Study Center after school for MTC students with volunteer teachers assisting;

establishing an Academic Fellowship Program from external sources for at-risk students as financial incentives for maintenance of school grades;

the incorporation of Limited English Proficient students into MTC with support from a grant form the Federal Office of Education, Bilingual Division;

the development of curriculum changes for MTC students through cooperative planning by program teachers and university faculty;

the use of Peer Resource Training program at San Francisco State University to train STC graduates who are now college freshmen as peer resources to return to their high school to work with ninth graders.

Mission To College began with a small core of four or five teachers who shared the administrators' belief that many of Mission's students should be college bound. In its second year, this core grew to twenty five as increasing numbers of teachers and students believed that many Mission students were capable of graduating and attending college and, therefore, should be in MTC.

Conditions and Opportunities

The conditions that enabled STC and MTC programs to develop were not unique to Mission High School. Many schools share in these characteristics, but a key factor was the confluence of these conditions and personalities at that school and how the key players viewed the opportunity to address a problem at hand. Their response, in turn, created more opportunities for proactive, strategic planning not only for continued management and development of the programs, but for other aspects of schooling that impacted on the student success.

For example, while MTC was developed as a way to teach students before they become seniors when they get a taste of university work, the search to ensure that students will have the requisite skills and courses for college track led many MTC teachers to explore various student groupings and methods for instruction. The school's curriculum, the ways students were grouped for instruction and how they were taught were brought to question by MTC teachers. As schools are like ecological systems (Eisner, 1988), MTC teachers' experimentation in curriculum and instruction addressed the 'regularities of schooling' which affected the larger student body (Goodlad, 1984).

There were several factors which were significant to the development of STC and MTC. These factors also created opportunities for proactive response. They include: a realistic opportunity to initiate action that will have impact on a major school problem; a shared recognition and understanding of the major school problem and a shared vision of what is possible for the students; the compatibility of key personalities and the trust that developed among them; the willingness to take risks, and the supportive environment that enabled key participants to take risks; the ability of the principal to establish an administrative structure that guided and supported the programs; and the ability of principal to garner resources inside and outside of school to support the programs. In the remainder of this section, these factors will be discussed in relation to the development of the programs and how they contribute to the administrator's ability to make proactive decisions.

A realistic opportunity

The beginning of Step To College was an example of the way in which many ideas and programs take hold in a school and, to some degree, supports the description of schools as loosely coupled organizations (Weick, 1982). In many urban schools, there is a 'sea of problems out there' (Aramendia, 1990), and while the principal may want to deal with them all, he is usually able to address only the most pressing ones which can change from day to day.

In the case of Mission High School, the Principal and Vice Principal did not come into the school with focused vision to address the high drop-out rate and low college attendance of those who did graduate. On the contrary, the Principal stated that her 'vision just walked into the door' at her first meeting with the college professor from San Francisco State University (Aramendia, 1990). Both the Principal and Vice Principal were new to their administrative positions as well as to the school. During their first year at Mission their immediate concern was to 'calm the school down' and make the school *look* like a school. Their first priority was to make the school a safe and neutral ground between rival Hispanic gangs. Furthermore, they implemented an attendance and tardy policy in an attempt to get the students out of the halls and into classrooms. By their accounts, these two changes were the focus of their energies that first year. What, then, provided the impetus and created the fertile ground for Step To College?

A critical factor in the development of STC was the existence of a general openness on the part of these administrators to those around them, and to what was available to help them make one of the 'millions of problems' something that could realistically be addressed (Aramendia,

1990). What contributed to this perception that 'something really can be done about the problem' were three interactive factors: the compatibility of personalities of the key actors, the congruence of their vision or sense of what was needed and possible to be done to address the problem, and the perception of their impact of what was proposed on the students and the school staff. In their initial meetings with the college professor who was the outsider to the school, these 'screens' were used to identify the problem to be addressed, to determine what needed to be done and to assess the extent to which this opportunity was realistic.

Evident from the interviews with the Principal and Vice Principal was that the compatibility of key personalities was crucial to the birth of the STC program. To them, the idea was important, but equally important was *who* brought the information. In this case, the compatibility of the key personalities was dependent on the trust they had in each others' judgment, and their shared understanding of the underlying issues of the problem. For example, the Principal had felt that there were many individuals and groups who expressed interest in working in the schools but have their own agendas. As Principal, it was her responsibility to carefully screen outside offers to protect the school from possible intrusion and disruptions.

As a consequence, the Principal agreed to the meeting only on the basis of the Vice Principal's high recommendation of the professor and her trust in the Vice Principal's judgment: 'He was someone I looked up to as my mentor. He cares about kids' (Tiernan, 1989). After their initial meeting, her confidence in her Vice Principal was bolstered by the Principal's own assessment that the professor indeed 'understood schools, our constraints, how high schools are run, and how our district operates' (Tiernan, 1989).

What also came forth in those initial meetings was the sense that there was agreement on what was a crucial problem of the school and a shared understanding of what was needed or possible to solve that problem. All three individuals knew that Mission had a large number of students not graduating and going to college. More importantly, as they talked, it was clear that they shared a common belief in and vision of what was possible for the students. On the basis of this shared vision, their focus became clear — how to get the kids into college — and they were free to brainstorm ideas and the 'program pieces fell into place' (Aramendia, 1990). As the program began to take shape, this commitment to the goal of the program was the driving force in determining what decisions were made and the nature of the process for making these decisions.

A final factor that contributed to the administrators' perception that the conditions presented a realistic opportunity to address a significant school problem was the extent to which the proposed idea or program contributed to their sense of what is good for the school. Key questions that concerned the principal included: Does it help my school? It is going to help the kids? What effect will it have on my teachers? Is it going to make the school look good?

Another important question reflected the Principal's concern for the degree of impact of proposed programs or change efforts on her teaching staff: How would the teachers receive this? Having been trained as a counselor (and, indeed, assigned as counselor at the high school in previous years before returning to the school as its Principal), she viewed the teachers as her caseload (Aramendia, 1990). A major concern was how the teachers would respond to the proposed efforts. The greater the disruption and changes demanded on the teachers, their schedules, attitudes and sense of well-being regarding their jobs and the school, the less likely the Principal would support the proposed program.

Underlying these questions was the Principal's perception of the central role she assumed in defining goals for her school. Her priority focus was on the specific needs of the students of the school rather than an automatic acceptance of the school district's goals as her school's goals. District goals and initiatives were evaluated in terms of their usefulness and impact on her school. Often times, they were recast to be consistent with what she perceived to be important goals for her school.

Believing that she and her administrative team were in the best position to identify areas of needed improvement, she assumed the responsibility of sorting out ideas presented to her from within as well as from outside the school. She would initiate action only on those that were determined to be consistent with the school's goals. 'I don't want someone to come in with a plan or program. They must be willing to come in and work *with* us, see what *we* do, and make support available to us' (Aramendia, 1990).

This manner of assessing potential opportunities of school involvement in change efforts and her sense of being a key articulator of the school's goals supports a proactive orientation to school administration. Hall and others have attributed these behaviors to principals having an 'initiator' style in facilitating change in schools (Hall *et al.*, 1984). The administrators applied this crucial screen in assessing the compatibility and promise of Step To College.

Risk taking

Once the opportunity presented itself as a realistic option to adddress a major problem of the school, the administrators and the college professor were willing to take the risk to initiate action and launch the program. Behind the willingness to take the risk on STC was the deep and shared conviction that something must be done about the high drop-out rate and low college attendance of their students.

As they brainstormed ideas on what to do, they focused on ways in which the resources of the university can be made available to the high school. Feeling that there was nothing to lose, they were willing to explore many ideas, drawing upon their collective experiences from working with Hispanic students as well as their understanding of Hispanic culture and needs of the families. For example, the Principal's past counseling experience led her to believe that the program must be offered to the students where they were, on the high school campus, because Hispanic parents would not allow their children to travel away from their neighborhood to the university. Their commitment to 'do whatever [they] can to make it possible for the students to get into college' led them to explore how traditional school and university policies, structures and practices can be modified and expanded to facilitate (Tiernan, 1989).

The resultant program was small, involving only forty seven seniors at the school, affecting only the one teacher whose classroom was used for the after school university course, and the school custodian whose good will was tapped to break routine and clean that classroom twice that day. The university modified their admission policy and allowed waiver of the application fee and tuition of these seniors.

The program was developed without any money and therefore did not have a budget. As a result, these three initiators of the program felt no constraints that dictated the shape of the program. They felt free to try whatever they wished, dictated only by the desire to fit the program to the needs of the students. With the Principal's 'dynamic spirit', the three 'seized the moment' and launched Step To College one semester after they met. Their risk taking made STC a unique initiative in academic retention programs.

Aministrative structure, attitudes and practices
A significant factor to the development, evolution and success of STC and MTC programs was the nature of the administrative team and how it functioned to support these programs. The make-up of the leadership for STC and MTC was significant in enabling MTC to serve as an ongoing, programmatic vehicle for forward planning and timely response to the problems of the school. Influential in this process were the Principal's perception of her role in relation to the teachers, the qualities she sought and valued in her fellow administrators, the importance of complementarity in abilities of her administrative team, her commitment and the clarity of the program goals which were shared by her administrative team members.

The Principal perceived her most important task to be building a strong administrative team. Foremost in building a strong team was identifying the 'good people' who would do what was needed for the school. 'Good people' were those with positive human relations skills, who shared the Principal's philosophy of handling people in conflict in a way that everyone wins in the situation. They must also be able to handle problems so that they do not escalate (Aramendia, 1989). She also sought in her administrators a sensitivity to, and an ability to relate to and understand, the particular experiences and needs of the students. For example, she sought to add an individual to her team who was highly respected as a classroom teacher by fellow teachers, who related well with students, and whose background was similar to a growing minority population of her school.

Crucial to getting the best people possible for the school was knowing who to call for their opinions regarding possible candidates and the willingness to do whatever was necessary to get the desired persons. Sometimes, it may require utilizing individuals or groups with the ability to place pressure on district decision makers and the process. The willingness to fight for or keep the best individuals on the team was based on the belief that as Principal, she, and not those outside the school, was most knowledgeable about who can best 'fit in' with the team and serve the needs of the school.

In addition to the ability to get the best people possible for the school, the Principal's ability to 'get the right horse in the right stall' was a significant factor of this administrative organization (Aramendia, 1989). The Principal believed that the complex nature of problems confronting urban schools demanded that her administrative team be able to function in a complementary manner in relation to each other. For example, her Vice Principal's strength in writing ability complemented her weakness in that area. Having identified individuals who possessed key characteristics that were valued, the Principal placed in them a great deal of trust that they would do their jobs.

Having key individuals identified in the school, a type of leadership team evolved for MTC teachers and two consultants outside the school. Each team member or entity assumed different roles and functions based on particular skills and interests of each member and the resources available to them from their unique positions in relation to the school organization. However, the leadership was not diffuse nor fragmented. Guided by clear goals of the program, a shared commitment to these goals, a recognition of each other's areas of expertise and responsibilities and an acceptance of a shared decision-making process, the relationship of the team members created a dynamic interaction that held the team together to yield a decisive collective leadership (Hall and Hord, 1986).

Such a school culture allowed for different levels of leadership, emerging from throughout the school organization (Ogawa and Bossert, 1989). Operating much like 'change facilitating' as described by Hall and Hord, members of the leadership team possessed sufficient knowledge and maintained consistent communication with each other such that 'the actions and the effects of each builds upon the actions and effects of the other' (Hall and Hord, 1986). The effect was a collective leadership that was greater than a mere sum of its separate members' efforts. For example, the Vice Principal, an Hispanic woman with immigrant experience not unlike many of the students, assumed the role of recruiting, identifying the students and communicating with their parents about STC and MTC. Her role in socializing the students to the responsibilities and expectations of the programs was key to changing student self-perceptions and setting the tone of the programs.

Programmatic and curricular issues were the domain of the core of MTC teachers whose classrooms served as the key arena for interaction with the MTC students and a crucial point of transmission of the skills and knowledge that the students needed to be college bound. Planning meetings' agenda emerged from the successes and trials of MTC teachers' interaction with students. The shape and substance of the program were decided by the teachers with the support of the administrators. More importantly, MTC teachers 'acted as ambassadors' (Tiernan, 1989) through talking and involving fellow teachers about the program, inviting their participation and gaining legitimacy for the program.

The Vice Principal, along with the MTC coordinator, maintained day-to-day contact with the teachers and facilitated communication and support. In contrast, the Principal played a major role in identifying the program as one of great importance for the school. One way she emphasized its importance was to remove some responsibilities from the Vice Principal and make STC and MTC her major responsibility. Her assigned responsibilities were absorbed by grants which enabled MTC teachers to travel and visit other school districts for program ideas and secured substitutes to release teachers from classrooms for planning.

Most interesting was the Principal's approach and perception of her role in relation to her teachers in change efforts. The Principal believed that change comes from the 'best people' (Aramendia, 1990) in the school: those who have the interests and needs of the students at heart, who have ideas and willingness to actualize these ideas. Looking around her staff for these people, the Principal would share her ideas and tried to get them 'excited about them, trust [them], and let them do what they want to do. Then it's my job to support them like crazy and start putting good pieces together' (Aramendia, 1990). 'Good pieces' involved securing funds, materials, and linking related and supportive programs from within and outside the school. One such example was the situation in which the Principal observed a group of teachers attempting to plan during their preparation period, but constantly running out of time. This led her to seek out and write a grant proposal to secure funds for substitutes in order to release teachers from classrooms for planning.

Because of the differentiated roles and responsibilities that each of the leadership team possessed, these same individuals became the students. They each function at major points of contact for the MTC program: the Vice Principal with recruitment and communication of students and parents, the MTC teachers with the students in the learning environment, the outside consultants with external monetary resources as well as access to current educational and instructional resources. 'You are as good as your information. You must have good people who are your eyes and ears, who are in touch with what's going on' (Aramendia, 1989).

As a group, they have become the change force for the school. By the nature of their positions, the Principal trusts the information they identify. Utilizing the existing structure of leadership, the leadership team were able to assess relevant information in order to plan and develop ways to address potential problems.

Driven by the main program question of what can be done to improve the delivery of curriculum to MTC students to ensure student success, MTC teachers, with the steady support of the Vice Principal and Principal, took on 'risky and gutsy' approaches (Tiernan, 1989). For example, teachers teaching honors and gifted classes explored ways to integrate their classes with MTC classes because MTC students were identified as having academic potential. The math department took the initiative to secure a grant that will enable them to explore various instructional approaches which were responsive to the cultural learning styles of the students.

Furthermore, as MTC teachers experimented with different and more effective ways to teach, they recognized the need for more frequent dialogue with fellow teachers who shared the same group of students. As the need and frequency for sharing curricular concerns and ideas increased, the desire to 'core' the students for instruction came from the teachers. What resulted was increased dialogue across grade levels and disciplines.

In another example of how MTC had served to identify emerging student problems, teachers found that because MTC did not take the 'cream' of the students but attempted to work with all students deemed to have college potential, some of these students were still 'at risk' of dropping out of school because pressures affecting their class performance continued to exist. Within the structure of MTC leadership, a possible solution that emerged was to develop a new class, possibly a 're-entry' class for those MTC students who needed to address specific problems that were beyond the control and training of teachers, but must be addressed because they stand in the way of the students' academic achievement. This class would offer specific remedies for the students and, in effect, expand the safety net to support those students who were at risk but have potential. This latest proposal emerged as a natural course of action arising from the operation and focus of MTC.

Securing resources
Possibly the most proactive behavior exhibited by the Principal in relation to the MTC program was her unique sense for identifying funds and her ability to adapt them to support the specific aspects of the program. This refined skill was rooted in her perception of her role as one of

'scouting around and finding what little [she] has control over and use it' to support the program (Aramendia, 1990). Any money secured for the program had direct impact in the program, in form of substitutes for teachers, salary for peer tutors, program coordinator, or teacher inservice costs.

An excellent example of identifying and linking existing funds within the school to support MTC was the use of the peer resource person already available at the school. Funded by the school district to direct specific activities for peer interaction, the peer resource person functioned differently at various sites. Here, the peer resource person was brought into the MTC program as coordinator of the buddy program that utilized college bound STC seniors as peer role models and a peer source of motivation and support. Such a program engendered a sense of caring and responsibility on the part of the upper clansmen to be examples as well as providing an opportunity for them to help address a major school problem. Particularly for schools with high minority student population, such activities create a climate of community which is consistent with and validates the orientation toward success found in many minority cultures. Thus, the MTC buddy program served as a powerful instrument for changing the cultural environment of the school.

The Principal's ability in knowing how to secure outside resources was significant in providing support to the program. For example, after the initial year of success with STC, it was clear that a program should be developed to funnel students into STC earlier than their junior year. MTC was created in response, but there were no funds to initiate or support the idea. About this time, a non-profit organization, Achievement Council, had contacted the Principal. While this organization had a specific approach in assisting principals of urban schools in 'turning around' the academic achievement of schools, the Principal saw the opportunity to link the Achievement Council in ways that supported MTC whose goals were already established.

The funds from the Council have enabled MTC to move out of the constraints of the given school budget and allowed the teachers to be exposed to the current and latest curricular and instructional approaches. Combined with their expertise in the classroom, they became the key source and decision makers of MTC's curricular innovations. It was the funds from the Council that supported visits of MTC teachers to other school districts to learn about successful programs and to get ideas for MTC. These funds continued to bring innovative individuals and the latest research to inservice teachers. These funds also supported meeting time for MTC teachers to discuss and plan.

In another example of the administrators' ability to adapt outside funds to the needs of MTC students, the funds were to be used to assist minority students to secure part-time employment. Finding that many minority students were reluctant to utilize their services, the agency approached the school. Reflecting real understanding of their students, the administrators recognized the nature of the problem as one where many of the MTC students sought minimum wage jobs after school to help supplement their family's income. As a consequence, many do not do well academically due to the lack of time for study.

Committed to the goals of MTC, the administrators redefined the job for the MTC students; their job was to study. Creatively, the funds were made available to support the increase of students' academic study time. The Academic Fellow grants allow the students to substitute work at low paying jobs with the job to study, three days a week after school with the assistance of tutors from classroom teachers and former STC, now university students. A year after Academic Fellow program began, the number of MTC students with improved grades and on the school's honor roll has increased. Significantly, a shift in value orientation has taken place among the students themselves. Non-MTC students began to attend the study center and availed themselves of the tutoring services.

In yet another example of the Principal's attentiveness in pulling resources to support MTC, the availability of math tutors from a nearby business college was put into place with the Academic Fellows' study center. Once again, the resource was used in ways to ensure the academic success of the students.

Conclusion

Together, the Step To College and Mission To College programs exemplified an encompassing program that can serve to be a vehicle for proactive decision making in addressing major concerns and needs of students. Not an isolated program benefiting a small, select group of students, it has become a pivotal program for connecting other programs of the school, in effect moving the total school towards its program goal of ensuring the academic success of students. Factors significant to its development help create an implementation process that was uniquely dynamic and interactive; where ideas, activities and approaches used to reach programmatic goals were constantly tested and refined. This enabled MTC to become a vehicle for identifying current and emerging school problems, for analyzing and assessing the information, and for exploring and developing possible solutions.

Foremost of the programs' characteristics was shared vision or belief among its leadership team in what was possible for the students. Bolstering this belief was the conviction to do whatever they can to help the student improve academically and be given the opportunity to attend the university. Toward this effort, the STC program was pushing the limits of the existing school structure for the students. As MTC developed and evolved in its attempts to grapple with basic, underlying problems affecting the students' low achievement, it effected change on the school's organizational structure, on the curriculum and instructional approaches of the school, and delineated the nature of collaborative relationships between the school and outside resources and agencies. These changes, in turn, allowed the administrators and the staff to become the central driving force for change, through a collective, reflective and dynamic process for responding to the changing needs of the school.

Key Points

1 Within a complex organizational structure, proactive decision making can evolve from a reactive environment.
2 Proactive decision making can initially create conflict in a dysfunctional organization.
3 A proactive leader must identify preliminary support personnel who provide the shared decision making, and additional information sources necessary to make meaningful decisions. After a period of time, additional personnel can be involved in the decision-making process.
4 Through the socialization process, proactive decision making can be transferred from the principal to the other teachers, students and community members.

Discussion Questions

1 Did the programs Step To College and Mission To College begin as a proactive effort? Please explain.
2 How would you define the type of leadership displayed at Mission High School?
3 What information sources were identified by the administration staff at Mission High School as they defined the problem and identified a course of action?
4 In retrospect how do you think they would have approached their planning differently?
5 What type of leadership do you think would have been more appropriate at Mission High School in organizing their plan of action? Please explain.

References

ARAMENDIA, P. (1989) Personal interviews.
ARAMENDIA, P. (1990) Personal interviews.

CUMMINS, J. (1986) 'Empower minority students: A framework for intervention', *Harvard Educational Review*, **56**, 1, pp. 18–36.

EISNER, E. (1988) 'The ecology of school improvement', *Educational Leadership*, February, pp. 24–9.

GOODLAD, J.I. (1983) 'The school as a workplace', in GRIFFIN, G. (Ed.) *Staff Development*, 82nd Yearbook of the National Society for the Study of Education, Part 2, Chicago, University of Chicago Press.

GOODLAD, J.I. (1984) *A Place Called School*, New York, McGraw-Hill.

HALL, G. and HORD, S. (1987) *Change in Schools*, Albany, State University of New York Press.

HALL, G. and HORD, S. (1986) *Configurations of School-Based Leadership Teams*, National Institute of Education R & D Report 3223.

HALL, G., RUTHERFORD, W., HORD, S. and HULING, L. (1984) 'Effects of three principal styles on school improvement', *Educational Leadership*, February, pp. 22–9.

OGAWA, R.T. and BOSSERT, S. (1989) 'Leadership as an organizational quality', unpublished paper presented at AERA Annual Meeting, San Francisco, March.

OLSEN, L. (1988) 'The restructuring puzzle', *Education Week*, November, p. 7.

PEREA, J.E. (1989) 'The Step To College Program at San Francisco State University', unpublished manuscript.

San Francisco Chronicle (1990) 'Urban schools providing more social services', 12 February.

SERGIOVANNI, T.J. and CORBALLY, J.E. (Eds) (1986) *Leadership and Organizational Culture: New Perspectives on Administrative Theory and Practice*, Urbana, University of Illinois Press.

TIERNAN, L. (1989) Personal interviews.

TIMAR, T. (1989) 'The politics of school restructuring', *Phi Delta Kappan*, December, pp. 266–75.

WEICK, K. (1982) 'Administering education in loosely coupled schools', *Phi Delta Kappan*, June, pp. 673–6.

Section Two: Administrative Computer Information Systems
Hal Jonsson

Jonsson teaches the required computing course for the Educational Administration credential and Master's Degree program at San Francisco State University. He is currently completing a study of resources available for computer-based technology courses offered to meet the computing competency requirements for teacher credential candidates in California institutions of higher education. The study is funded by the California State Department of Education through the California Technology Project, California State University.

Introduction

News media, professional education journals and social studies textooks proclaim that:

> With the widespread use of microcomputers and telecommunication, the information age is finally here. Inexpensive microcomputers are taking over many tasks formerly requiring expensive mainframe or minicomputers. Microcomputers are becoming much more user friendly. We expect to see a microcomputer on every teacher's and administrator's desk by 1991.

School site principals often respond:

> I'm hoping to retire before I need to learn to use a computer.

> New vice principals and some in the counseling group need to be able to use a computer, and the secretarial staff, but not experienced principals like me.

> Those people downtown have time for that management information stuff, we've got too much front line pressure to play around with computers.

The importance of current, comprehensive and objective information on which to base administrative decision making cannot be overstated. Computer technology is making possible the addition of the most influential new tools for providing information. In the business world this branch of computing is called MIS (Management Information Systems). The survival and growth of new firms, and the demise of seemingly well-established ones, is often associated with the quality of their MIS departments. The relevance of MIS to educational settings has been advanced by several authors (Tanner and Holmes, 1985; Faux, 1986; Bank and Williams, 1987; Richards, 1989).

In this section, we are first introduced to the type of computer applications which are commonly associated with administrative computing at the school level. Most of these are familiar, in the sense that they are simply more efficient ways of accomplishing tasks which formerly were carried out much more slowly by administrators and support personnel.

In middle and secondary schools, many principals, vice principals, head counselors, and clerks worked for several weeks, often during summers, completing the master schedule, student scheduling, and student records. There tasks usually can now be accomplished in a few hours. (Although at the beginning stages, it must be admitted, learning how to use new computer equipment and applications can often seem like a formidable and time-consuming endeavor.)

After introducing a few applications for the school site level, a spreadsheet example relating to district level and teacher organizations is presented. This followed by a proposal to broaden the perspective about administrative computing to encompass a more comprehensive set of functions and a more interactive, dynamic character, somewhat in line with effective MIS in the business world. This proposal is particularly relevant to the theme of this book, in that it makes possible the timely information base that is usually a prerequisite to more proactive administrative decision making.

As an example of a recently established implementation of an administrative computer information system that embodies a broader scope and more interactive, dynamic functions, the one for San Francisco Unified School District is presented in substantial detail. We will examine features that apply individually at the classroom, school, and district levels, and then jointly, and with interactive potential between classroom and school, between school and district, and between classroom and district. Finally we will consider briefly some options available to school districts which have not begun to move into distributed computing at the school site level.

Readers familiar with school site administrative work will no doubt recognize that most of the following computer applications and/or administrative tasks are relevant to the professional responsibilities of principals and school support staff:

Word processing

Data base management

Spreadsheets

Telecommunications

Desktop publishing

Student records

Attendance

Master scheduling

Student scheduling

Grade reporting

Course history and transcripts

Test scoring and test score recording.

When justifying the outlays for computer equipment, software, and the training required in using these applications, the most obvious rationale that comes to mind is the one of increased productivity. Certificated and classified personnel are now able to accomplish in considerably less time established tasks that were formerly done with more labor intensive methods and less efficient equipment.

If pressed for additional justification for using these computer applications, educators who are familiar with their use can rightfully claim that output for several established tasks can be improved with computer use. Printed products look better, contain fewer errors, and are more personalized.

Timely Information Production

Obtaining information quickly can assist in more effective administrative action in established areas of responsibility. Some of the computer applications listed above can easily produce this more timely information.

Attendance reporting

A well publicized type of example is attendance reporting at the middle and high school levels. With the rapid turn-around times made possible with the use of mark sense period attendance, teachers, counselors, and administrators can have very up-to-date attendance reports. When these reports serve as input to manual or automatic telephone dialing equipment, parents can usually be notified the same day. Many school districts have found that this technology, especially when combined with a follow-through individualized counseling program, significantly reduces truancy rates, and more than pays for itself with increased ADA and reduced dropout rates.

School site department budgets

At the school site level, spreadsheets can be designed so that summary screens are automatically linked to subsidiary sections in such a way that any change in a subsidiary account will be instantaneously reflected in the summary screens. In the example seen in Table 4.1, the summary screen for department expenditures is linked to each department's account. Thus an administrator can tell at a glance the current financial status of any department as well as that for the entire school with regard to this budget category.

Andrew E. Dubin

Table 4.1   Spreadsheet for department budgets (abbreviated)

UTOPIA HIGH SCHOOL 1990–91

Department Equipment, Supplies, Repairs, and Miscellaneous Budget Report.
Total Allocation: $64,500

1 Nov 1990	Allocated Tot	Exp	Encmbr	Exp & Enc	Balance
Art	3870	2120	580	2700	1170
Business	5160	3760	720	4480	680
Cons/Fam/Diet	5160	1085	1140	2225	2935
Computing	7740	3475	3035	6510	1230
English	5160	1580	1020	2600	2560
Foreign Langs	4515	2220	500	2720	1795
Hist/Soc Sci	4515	1580	1020	2600	1915
Indust Arts	5160	1870	400	2270	2890
Mathematics	4515	1550	470	2020	2495
Music	7740	3030	200	3230	4510
Sciences	10965	3795	530	4325	6640
Total all Depts	64500	26065	9615	35680	28820

1 Nov 1990	Allocated Tot	Exp	Encmbr	Exp & Enc	Balance
Art	3870	2120	580	2700	1170
brushes		300	100		
canvas		300	50		
clay		370	40		
paint		500	0		
software		650	390		
miscellaneous		0	0		

1 Nov 1990	Allocated Tot	Exp	Encmbr	Exp & Enc	Balance
Business	5160	3760	720	4480	680
equip. rep.		800	200		
paper		600	400		
ribbons		900	120		
software		1460	0		
miscellaneous		0	0		

Note: The accounts of individual departments are shown only for Art and Business.

The crucial difference between a well-designed spreadsheet and a comparable manual bookkeeping system is the dynamic linkage between and among the various components. As soon as permitted change is made in one component it can be reflected in other components.

Comparison of teacher grading
As suggested and illustrated by Richards (1989, p. 18) spreadsheets can easily be applied to checking for grade inflation and for differences among teachers in their overall grading standards. In the example illustrated in Table 4.2 the grade averages for different English teachers for a succession of academic years is entered in a spreadsheet format, and the means

Table 4.2   English teachers' annual grade averages for required courses for 1986–90 academic years

Teacher	Grade Level	1986	1987	1988	1989	1990	Means of Individual Teacher Averages
Barnes	9	2.52	2.71	2.61	2.87	2.95	2.73
Jones	9	2.34	2.44	2.57	2.42	2.57	2.47
Larson	10	2.83	3.05	2.98	3.14	3.16	3.03
Funk	10	2.27	2.42	2.35	2.53	2.49	2.41
Davis	11	3.05	2.93	3.14	3.25	3.32	3.14
Rogers	11	2.38	2.46	2.33	2.56	2.63	2.47
Yearly mean averages		2.57	2.67	2.66	2.80	2.85	

(arithmetic averages) of the averages are calculated using the built-in formulas of the spreadsheets. If needed, more formal statistical significance tests could also be carried out using formulas provided in most spreadsheets. The trends of teacher grade averages over the five years are uniformly up, and the differences among the means of the averages of the individual teachers are quite substantial. Undoubtedly, this spreadsheet display could serve to focus the attention of interested parties on the issues of grade inflation and differences among teacher grading practices.

Most spreadsheets also have graphing capability. The yearly means for each teacher could also be displayed on a line graph to illustrate the trends. Bar graphs would serve to illustrate differences among the means of individual teacher grade averages.

District and teacher organization salary bargaining

A spreadsheet application which is not publicized much (but which is commonly used by school districts in their budget planning and by school districts and professional organizations in salary bargaining) is illustrated, in abbreviated form, in Table 4.3. This type of spreadsheet design allows districts and organizations to evaluate immediately the effect on the salary schedule and on the total of teacher's salaries, of any proposed change in BASE. The conventional teachers' salary schedule can be extracted from this type of spreadsheet by printing it to a word-processing file and eliminating the irrelevant rows. The salary schedule information is in the Step rows. The BASE salary amount, the multipliers, and number of teachers at each step are there in the example as place holders only, and are used to make it easy to check on the correctness of the spreadsheet design.

It is only slightly more difficult to design a spreadsheet with the same appearance but which would work in reverse, in that it would allow

Table 4.3 Spreadsheet for teacher salaries (abbreviated)

School District Teacher Salary Schedule with Step and Column Multipliers, Number of Teachers at Each Step, Step Subtotals, and Total Teachers' Salaries (Designed with formulas for starting with BASE SALARY entry. BASE Salary entry: $20,000.)

Seniority Steps	Degree(s) and Units Columns	1	2	3	
	Semest. Units	AB	AB + 30	AB + 60	Step Subtotals
Step 1	Multiplier	1.00	1.10	1.20	
	Salary	20,000	22,000	24,000	
	No. of Tchrs	2	2	2	
	Slry Subtots	40,000	44,000	48,000	132,000
Step 2	Multiplier	1.15	1.25	1.35	
	Salary	23,000	25,000	27,000	
	No. of Tchrs	2	2	2	
	Slry Subtots	46,000	50,000	54,000	150,000
Step 3	Multiplier	1.30	1.40	1.50	
	Salary	26,000	28,000	30,000	
	No. of Tchrs	2	2	2	
	Slry Subtots	52,000	56,000	60,000	168,000
Grand Total for District Teachers' Salaries					$450,000

the initial input to be the grand total for district teachers' salaries. It would then generate all the dollar amounts from the one input. This would allow school districts and professional organizations to experiment with the effect on the salary schedule of various adjustments in row and column multipliers. Of course, this assumes that there is agreement about the amount of the grand total available for teachers' salaries.

As was stated above, what makes this type of spreadsheet so effective is the dynamic linkage among the various components, and the speed with which a permitted change in one is reflected in the others. Also 'hard copies' can be printed very quickly and circulated for discussion. This can reduce last minute surprises at the bargaining table.

More Comprehensive Educational Management Information Systems

A less obvious and more comprehensive type of school site and school district computer use relates to what in the business community is called Management Information Systems or MIS. These systems, when properly designed and implemented, can provide much more timely information, as well as new types of information for administrative operations and especially for decision making. Frank, Mackett, Abrams, and Nowakowski have concluded that current pressures for school improvement are forcing educational administrators 'to manage student achievement and staff performance more effectively while maintaining fiscal stability of the educational system' (Frank *et al.*, 1986, p. 95).

They propose that in order to meet this challenge, new information systems are required that include and integrate the following components:

Student management

Personnel management

Instructional management

Fiscal management

Organizational management

Information management.

In a different publication, these same authors, (Mackett *et al.*, 1988, p. 237) recommend that planning and development be implemented to determine the characteristics of information systems that can effectively accomplish the integration of these components, most of which they claim exist in some form in a variety of school districts throughout the country. They also recommend preservice and inservice training for prospective and current school administrators in the use of new and integrated school management information systems.

An Integrated Computerized Information System for a Large School District

The design of the computerized information system, which is presented in this section as an example of such an integrated system, has been developed in the San Francisco Unified School District over a period of years. The handling of centralized services such as payroll was computerized in the early 1960s using a mainframe computer. In the late 1960s experimentation at a few secondary sites involving terminals and minicomputers was begun (Harrington, 1989).

In the late 1970s and early 1980s several teachers helped pioneer the use of microcomputers in the classroom, but it was not until the mid-1980s that consistent policies of hardware and software selection for the 'micros' were implemented at the classroom and school site level.

In the mid-1980s also, a new superintendent, Ramon Cortines, instituted in the district a system of Management by Objectives. Each year, as in most districts, the school board approves the overall goals and objectives and all staff and site planning in the district is directed towards the achievement of these goals and objectives.

As the goals and objectives included such universal ones as 'the improvement of student achievement', 'improving class attendance', and 'reducing drop-outs', it became obvious that a district management information system was needed that could provide continuing feedback to school site administrators, counselors, and teachers and to district administrative personnel about progress in these areas.

At about the same time the district was involved in litigation concerning the status of ethnic integration in several schools. A court decision created what has come to be known as the 'consent decree schools', a set of elementary schools, middle schools, and high schools, whose enrollment has to be closely monitored with regard to ethnic makeup. Part of the consent decree stipulation also provided that these schools would become magnet schools, in part by offering students and faculty special resources and training in computing to attract and hold a more ethnically balanced student population.

The need for additional and timely information at the district level combined with the additional school site office and classroom computer resources has provided the stimulus for the development of a coherent information system which includes the use of computers at classroom, school office, and district office levels.

The design of this information system is presented in the form of a conventional Venn diagram of three overlapping circles, with one representing classrooms, another school offices, and a third the district office. The meaning of the labels in the diagram, especially the acronyms or abbreviations, needs elaboration.

Category Circles, Exclusive of Intersections (Figure 4.1)

Classroom
The general theme of *integration into curriculum* of the use of micros is quite well known. Collis (1988) has spelled out the rationale and presented detailed plans for implementation in each of several curriculum areas. In the San Francisco Unified School District the potential for implementation, especially in the 'consent decree' schools, has gone considerably beyond what Collis envisions because of the additional mandated computer and staff development resources.

School office
The use of micros, IBM AT type, in the school office facilitates the expeditious accomplishment of several functions that previously have been done tediously by pencil and paper, or on terminals connected to mini or mainframe computers, or which had simply not been done at all.

Scheduling: This vital activity can take place by downloading student information from MCIS (described below) from the central office and

*Figure 4.1 SFUSD Management Information System design with classroom, school office, and district office functions, **Exclusive of Intersections** (Harrington, 1989)*

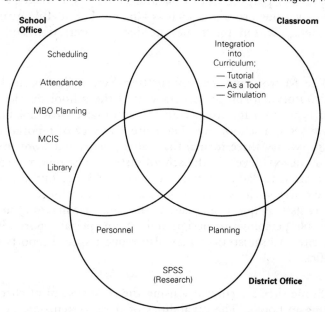

allows the shifting of student assignments and the printing of class lists at the school site. At the middle and high school levels a set of programs on the mainframe automates class scheduling at the beginning of each semester and then allows modifications and changes during the semester at the school site level using HEMLOCK (to be discussed later).

Attendance: At the middle and high school levels, period by period attendance is taken in all classes, and in some schools is entered by terminal into the mainframe. In other schools the data are 'scanned' on site and uploaded from micros. In either case, period by period attendance is available on all secondary students with reports of cutting and truancy available with very short turn-around times at school site and district levels.

MBO (Management by Objectives) planning: All principals are required to submit site plans for carrying out the goals and objectives of the district for the current year. At some sites a system is being piloted which allows the entry of planned activities in a data base in parallel with the planned budget for carrying out the activities. The plans are then aggregated and reported to the program administrators in a variety of formats which allow the negotiations with the sites about annual budgets and their modifications to be driven by activities rather than by formulas and 'line items'. The tracking of budget expenses, (purchase order, requisitions, etc. at the site) can then be tied to the educational activities.

Balance can be maintained over the school year in more equitable fashion. A further purpose of this planning model is to make possible the alignment of various programs such as Chapter I, ESL-Bilingual, Special Education, etc., within the same site/district interaction and tracking system.

MCIS: The MicroComputer Information System has been developed by administrators and programmers within the school district, using a dBASE III type language, to permit the automated downloading of the student data set at a school site. There are a variety of reports (a total of sixty five in twenty three forms) that can be generated from menus that are useful at various levels in the school district. The reports provide not only information for administrative decision making, but also for more mundane services such as mailing labels, records of locker assignments, and birthday lists. A query language in the data base makes it possible for knowledgeable personnel to design and obtain special reports directly at the school site. Administrators may also request special reports from the district office.

Library: Some sites are currently using the code system of checking out and checking in books. The capabilities of these systems are being automated with the use of micros. In addition, some sites are experimenting with on-line searching of commercial data bases as an adjunct to the catalog/readers' guide type of reference search.

District office
The final separate category (circle) represents the central office uses of computers. Like most other large districts, early use was made of mainframe computers for automating payroll and personnel records.

Personnel: In addition to the obvious accounting functions connected with payrolls, all the record keeping for certification, in-service credits, and related functions are used by central office employees on the mainframe.

Planning: Management and record keeping of physical plant maintenance and improvements are totally computerized. The student data base is complete enough to be used for accurate enrollment projections. It is also used as input to two California State Department of Education data collection systems, one of which tracks student and site performance as part of the California Assessment Program, and the other which tracks the need for new construction.

The California Test of Basic Skills (CTBS), which is an individual test of student achievement, is very important to the district in tracking

Figure 4.2   SFUSD Management Information System design focusing on **Intersections** of classroom, school office, and district office functions (Harrington, 1989)

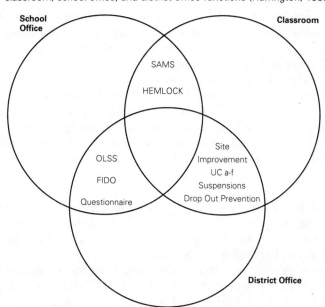

the progress of the 'stayer' students. These students are the ones that have continuous enrollment in our high transiency district.

The CTBS scores are analyzed for differences among the various ethnic groups, programs, schools, and grade levels. Reports based on these analyses are influential in administrative planning.

SPSS (a program for statistical analysis):   Studies are carried out on a variety of variables such as demographic characteristics, achievement, and attendance, which permit a clearer understanding of factors such as student groups 'at risk' for dropping out. Each year a District Profile is published which summarizes all the basic demographics, test scores, program availability, and budget information for each of about 130 district school sites. Any interested party can get an immediate overview of the status of each school in the district.

Intersections of the Three Category Circles (Figure 4.2)

Classroom with School Office Intersection
SAMS (Student Achievement Management System):   This system provides a Computer Managed Instruction (CMI) package using site-level micro-computers. It is tied to the MCIS system. SAMS can be used to produce the forms for multiple-choice answer sheets, to scan and score answer

sheets, and to track and process student test scores across hundreds of curriculum objectives.

In its full-blown application, SAMS is designed to provide curriculum, evaluation, and record keeping support for instruction that is organized on a 'targeted' or 'mastery' or 'outcome' basis, as well as a variety of other testing approaches.

The goal of the systems design is that once data have been entered, personnel at the site office, and eventually the district office, can track the achievement of students throughout the school year, instead of waiting for the once a year 'official results' on the standardized achievement test to tell administrators and the public 'how well the schools are doing'. The system is now being pilot tested at some elementary schools.

HEMLOCK: This system is designed at present to allow middle and high school administrators and counselors to use micros to schedule new and returning students, to keep running class balances, and provide more flexible solutions to scheduling conflicts *once* SOCRATES has done the batch job at the beginning of the semester.

Within a year or two this system will have the capability to handle the entire scheduling task at the school sites. (HEMLOCK will then have 'killed' SOCRATES.) Middle and high schools will then enjoy the benefits of a distributive system which will allow the complete scheduling operation to be carried out at the site level.

School office with district office intersection
OLSS (On Line Student Systems): About half of the school sites in the district currently have the capability to enroll new students directly through OLSS. This eliminates the entire cycle of paper forms and quickly allows the database to reflect actual student enrollment. The system allows for the simultaneous monitoring of ethnic balances in compliance with the court ordered integration plan, and the monitoring of class size and balance at the school site and district offices. The district is moving toward placing the necessary hardware at all school sites.

FIDO: This electronic bulletin board host system provides for the downloading of data from MCIS to the school site office. It also provides E-Mail exchange between the district office and school offices. Current plans call for the electronic publication of the Weekly Administrative bulletin (WAD) with a 'hypertext' database format in which it will be easier for an individual to find the relevant information than in the traditional hard copy.

Effective Schools Questionnaire: For more than three years an ever growing number of schools have been collecting data from a series of teacher opinion surveys based on the effective schools climate studies. These surveys have been customized to the needs and interests of each particular school using an on-site micro with access to an inventory of 1200 questions. The surveys have been designed at each site by a team of administrators and teachers after obtaining teacher responses to a short general questionnaire.

Orange County in California has been using a similar approach, but each school there has had to request the customization from the district level. SFUSD is adding items to the basic effective schools model set, especially in the areas of curriculum and multicultural education.

District office with classroom intersection
Site improvement: Site improvement is the individual school effort responding to the findings from the effective schools surveys and the data in the District Profile referred to under the SPSS heading above. The district is in the process of making available to interested parties at each school site, parents, students, teachers, and administrators, a range of base line data about student achievement, school climate, program availability, and budget information which will allow any individual at any level to respond to the mandate for school improvement in a constructive way.

UC a-f subject reports: The state university systems in California, as many other states, exert considerable influence on our high school curriculum by specifying prerequisite subject area course work which applicants must complete prior to admission. The district is tracking enrollments in these courses by ethnicity and reporting enrollments below expected levels for any group to the school site administrators, counselors, and teachers. Recruitment and support for underrepresented groups is vigorously encouraged.

Suspensions: Tracking and reporting of suspensions by ethnicity is being carried out on a regular basis. The district provides regular staff development work for administrators and counselors to find more effective and sometimes non-traditional disciplinary methods.

Dropouts: The use of centralized data collection and reporting about student behavior related to dropping out has provided the basis for administrative decisions about how to combat this problem faced by most large city school districts. The focus of efforts within SFUSD has been on the 15 per cent of students who account for 50 per cent of all cutting. The hypothesis behind this effort, confirmed by data analysis, is that it is among these 15 per cent of students that cutting leads to truancy, and frequently to dropping out. For this relatively small number of students, monthly reporting of cutting for each student is provided to administrators and counselors so that they can make extra efforts in

Figure 4.3 SFUSD Management Information System design showing the **Union** of classroom, school office, and district office functions (Harrington, 1989)

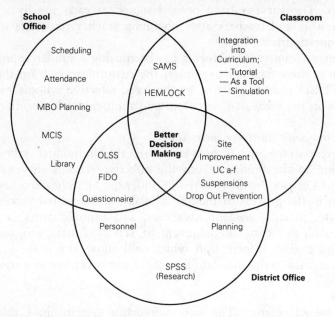

contacting the students and their families to decrease the cutting, and thus reduce the likelihood that they will drop out.

Summary

Administrative leaders in the San Francisco Unified School District view an effective management information system as made up of three overlapping, mutually reinforcing parts, covering respectively, the classroom, the school office, and district headquarters (see Figure 4.3). The technical backbone of this information system is the computer network and associated software, together with the technical expertise of the users. These parts must act in harmony to assist decision makers at all levels to solve problems, make better decisions, and better achieve the educational goals and objectives of the district and state.

Options for Districts Without Customized Mini or Mainframe Systems

As the trend toward distributed computing systems with powerful networked micros increases and the emphasis on school-centered decision making grows, comprehensive ready-made, modularized school administrative software packages have become available for school site use. Some also have the capability of connecting to micros or minicomputers at district headquarters, with additional modules designed specially for district headquarters applications.

An example of this type of system currently used in over ten per cent of California public schools and in several other states is SASI (School Administrative Student Information) from Educational Timesharing Systems, Orange, CA. The designers of SASI have evidenced a thorough understanding of the realities of education computing at the school and district levels.

Osiris from Tamarac Systems, Englewood, CO, is a similar system with many desirable features. Several other quality systems are available throughout the country (Bruder, 1988). Most include modules that are designed around specialized data base programs and which provide many of the features listed at the beginning of this section as being germane to the responsibilities of school site administrators and support staff, such as:

Student records

Attendance

Master scheduling

Student scheduling

Grade reporting

Course history and transcripts

Test scoring and test score recording

Local area networking

Telecommunications.

Merging of reports with major wordprocessing software
From an information management perspective it is especially important that a system have a flexible field name feature that allows custom fields to be added to a record design. It must have an easy-to-use telecommunication capability. Also the system must have a query language that makes it possible to generate reports that do not appear on the standard menu.

At the present time, most of the best microcomputer software systems run on IBM type micros of the 286, 386, or 486 series. With the availability in the Macintosh line of the more powerful Mac IIcx and IIci series, we will no doubt see more effective information systems software designed specifically for them, although the current list prices of this hardware are more expensive.

In addition to task features, ease of learning, networkability, cost, and expandability, it is important to consider the quality and cost of support and training provided by the vendor, also policies and established record of upgrades to modules in response to user requests.

Conclusion

So far, experience in many school districts indicates that installing a computerized management information system, in the form of micro-computer hardware, software, and skilled technical personnel, is only the first step in an evolutionary process that will continue to require a great deal of staff development work and increased professional preparation, not all of which focuses on fostering technical competence, or over-coming a quite common fear of computer technology (Wright, 1990).

Ultimately the use of these types of management information systems, whether custom deigned or more 'off the shelf', requires a change in the way administrative leaders conceptualize the basis and timing of decision making. A well-designed and carefully implemented system can provide more comprehensive, timely, objective, and widely available information on which to base administrative decisions, from the level of the classroom teachers and principal, to that of the district administrators. It can give teachers and administrators the tools to take a more proactive role at whatever level they have responsibility.

Note

1   The assistance of Dr Robert Harrington, Director of Evaluation, SFUSD, in this section is gratefully acknowledged.

Key Points

1   Technology is an extremely powerful tool to assist in proactive decision making.
2   A proactive decision maker must understand the available technology in order to apply it intelligently to his school site management strategies.
3   An expert support person at the school site can provide the proactive principal with the relevant information for program development, curriculum integration, scheduling and records to make substantive desisions.
4   A proactive principal must be aware of the current technology and what is anticipated for the future.

Discussion Questions

1   Please identify three different computer systems Jonsson cites and state to what area of the school program they would apply.
2   Based upon his review of computer information systems, do you feel schools can be more efficiently managed with their inclusion and in what ways?
3   What obstacles do proactive principals experience in utilizing some of the technology at the school site?
4   In what area should high technology replace personnel? How does a proactive decision maker initiate such a process?
5   Should technology be used in the development of all school information sources? In what area does technology not belong when considering the management of a school?

References

BANK, A. and WILLIAMS, R.C. (1987) *Information Systems and School Improvement: Inventing the Future*, New York, Teachers College Press.

BRUDER, I. (1988) 'Users speak out: A look at six administrative software programs', *Electronic Learning*, May/June, pp. 54–6.

COLLIS, B. (1988) *Computers, Curriculum, and Whole Class Instruction*, Belmont, Calif., Wadsworth Publishing Co.

FAUX, J. (1986) 'Emerging technologies in information management', in HENTSCHKE, G. (Ed.) *School Business Administration: A Comparative Perspective* Berkeley, Calif., McCutchan, Chapter 16.

FRANK, F., MACKETT, M., ABRAMS, P. and NOWAKOWSKI, J. (1986) 'The education utility and educational administration and management,' in GOOLER, D. (Ed.) *The Education Utility: The Power to Revitalize Education and Society*, Englewoods Cliffs, N.J., Educational Technology Publications, pp. 94–107.

HARRINGTON, R. (1989) 'San Francisco Unified Schools Policy Information System,' unpublished manuscript.

MACKETT, M., FRANK, F., ABRAMS, P. and NOWAKOWSKI, J. (1988) 'Computers and educational excellence: Policy implications for educational administration', in GRIFFITHS, D., STOUT, R. and FORSYTH, P. (Eds) *Leaders for American Schools: The Report and Papers of the National Commission on Excellence in Educational Administration*, Berkeley, Calif., McCutchan, Chapter 19.

POWGROW, S. (1984) 'Buying an attendance program', *Electronic Learning*, January, pp. 28–30.

RICHARDS, C.E. (1989) *Microcomputer Applications for Strategic Management in Education: A Case Study Approach*, New York, Longman, pp. 18–20.

TANNER, C. and HOLMES, C. (1985) *Microcomputer Applications in Educational Planning and Decision Making*, New York, Teachers College Press.

WRIGHT, K. (1990) 'The road to the global village', *Scientific American*, March, pp. 83–94.

Section Three: Supportive Supervision: Leadership for the Twenty-First Century
Stanley William Rothstein

The holder of a professorship in the Graduate Department of Educational Administration at California State University, Fullerton, Rothstein has also had many years of experience as a teacher and administrator in the New York City school system. He is the author of numerous refereed research articles in educational and social science journals and books, and publications in major newspapers, journals and media magazines. He is the author of two textbooks: *Leadership Dynamics: Advanced Perspectives in School Administration* and *Power to Punish*.

All staff members go through learning experiences or phases; all develop ways of doing things which are peculiarly their own. This happens the moment a new teacher or counselor enters his school. In the movement from a new staff member to someone who will become, in time, a veteran, his control structure or ego, undergoes a series of shocks and strains as it tries to deal with the problems of school life. Studies of this transitional period from student to teacher or counselor have shown us some of the difficulties (Rothstein, 1983). Exactly what happens to the ego of a staff person cannot be predicted. But certain control functions of the newcomer need to be supported by administrators and certain changes foreseen. All staff members and children deserve psychological and educational support. Each of them is going through socialization processes in order to become something other than what they are when they begin their schooling experiences: new teachers and counselors are moving away from their student identities toward that of the professional educator; children are in the long and arduous process of becoming adults. The control structure of individuals is deeply involved in all of these socializing and learning processes. Especially its cognition function needs to be strengthened if it is to perceive and understand school life correctly. What can administrators do to help the ego perform this important task for staff members? How can they help teachers and counselors to be in contact with one another and with their own innermost thoughts and feelings? Just what are some of the things a skilled supervisor needs to do in order to keep staff members on an even keel?

Researchers seem to feel that the total school climate must be the setting within which all support efforts are employed (Redl and Wineman, 1952). This includes weekly individual and group conferences. The 'how-to' of educational support takes place in regularly scheduled meetings where staff members are encouraged to verbalize their thoughts and feelings; where they are helped to identify and resolve problems which come up in their classrooms and guidance centers. The ego is strengthened in these meetings. Teachers and counselors become more aware of what is really happening in their interaction with one another and with students; their control functions are constantly flexed and strengthened. Why is it important for a teacher or counselor to admit he dislikes one of the students or fellow faculty members? Because, until he does, he may not be completely aware of these feelings or the reactions they are provoking in others. He may not be aware of the double messages being sent; or the deeper reasons for his own attitudes and behavior.

How does a supervisor know which people to talk about once he has begun the supervisory meeting? Several methods can be used. He can listen to the staff member and discuss those mentioned in the conversation, or ask what the teacher or counselor knows about each and every person they are working with. A teacher may be asked why he knows so much about Jane or Harry or why does he know so little about Stanley and Juan. How can he explain knowing so much about others? Are the children he knows little about 'outsiders' in their classrooms? And if they are, what is the counselor doing to help them make friends? What is he doing to integrate them into friendship groups? Too often, staff are not accepting them because they appear to be too shy and timid. Unbeknown to them, children are not accepting these children outside the classroom. They are not playing with them during recess when teachers often do not notice what is going on. And, too often, they fail to understand and support these newcomers adequately (Rothstein, 1981).

The very scheduling of weekly meetings where staff can reflect on and verbalize about their efforts and experiences provides an environment in which ego support and personality strengthening can take place. At the same time, it also requires that school administrators become more skilled and knowledgeable about how the control structures of individuals work; that they learn to help teachers and counselors to develop inner controls and insights into their own behavior and feelings.

Ego Function

Ego psychology had a mixed reputation until Anna Freud's classic works were published. And it is only in the last few years that there has developed a literature and technology based on ego psychological research and on the efforts of some to use these findings to solve interpersonal problems in modern organizations and society (Jacobson, 1964).

From what Anna Freud, Heinz Hartmann and others have discovered, and from what can be inferred from the work of Fritz Redl and others, the ego has a number of important functions which deserve attention. First, it is the task of the ego to help staff members, supervisors and students to understand the world around them. The ego makes assumptions about what things are like in the school and warns when there is danger. It estimates and calculates possibilities and consequences. 'I won't report to the dean's office,' says a boys's impulsive system, remembering what he has heard or experienced in such places. His ego may then interject itself: 'It isn't good to be late. Remember what the dean does to boys who don't report directly to his office.' It also summarizes the social situation that staff find themselves in. Here reference is made to the influence of primary groups an individual belongs to, as well as the rules and regulations of the school organization. When a person's urges and impulses threaten to conflict with the social norms and standards, the ego again provides warning signals about what could happen if such impulses were tranformed into behavior. The ego assesses the school world in which teachers and counselors must do their work, and it warns them of potential danger and unpleasantness when their urges threaten to come into conflict with the realities of school life. It discovers, it assesses and it seeks to learn what is happening in the outer world.

Another important function of the ego is to discover what is happening within the mind or impulsive system of an individual. Some contents of the impulsive system are not known to the control structure because they represent repressed emotions or are embedded in the unconscious. But if the ego does not know about them, how can it exercise its control function effectively? So the ego is continually engaged in searching out and monitoring the feelings, urges, impulses, anxieties and fears that cause an individual to behave in a particular way when he is unaware of this impulsive striving. Self-insight, then, is an important function of the control structure, or ego. It is also the task of the ego to become aware of the values which motivate an individual's behavior. Certain actions would not be accepted by a person's conscience or superego because of deep-seated beliefs about what is right and wrong, fair and unfair. But researchers have discovered that such values can be unconscious, too, and therefore, outside the knowledge and control of the ego. In such cases, the ego must ferret out these conscience-like admonitions, and the administrator's job is to become self-aware so he can help the staff person's ego to begin the process of cognition; so he can help him with anxieties and guilt feelings.

To the regulatory functions of the ego and superego can be added that of identity formations and self-esteem (Redl and Wineman, 1952). In these control centers impulsive energies can be balanced and neutralized, providing greater harmony between them and the social world of the individual. Self-esteem or acceptance is important because it determines how well a person can handle stress and crises, and how clearly he can hear and understand others. The person who has low self-esteem has had experiences in the past which portrayed him as an unworthy or incompetent person. Such an individual may come to see himself as deformed or abnormal in some way. He may doubt his abilities and intelligence and look to others for support and guidance. Or he may feel that all relationships will end unhappily, once others come to know him well. This explains why such individuals often distance themselves in order to guard against further rejection. The distortions this introduces into the communication process are considerable.

A person's self-esteem remains relatively constant; his feelings about the self remain the same in most situations. This means that such feelings are important factors in relationship building and in understanding the communication of others.

It also means that high self-esteem and acceptance is significant for administrators who want to hear and understand what others are saying to them. A surprising number of supervisors tend to think and act cynically toward themselves and others. Such attitudes and behavior undercut any support a school may undertake. A supervisor's health and psychological well-being depend, to a large degree, on the feelings he has about himself. If the supervisor sees himself as unworthy, incompetent, or worse, his perceptions will be negatively influenced by these feelings. Is he respected and well-liked? Do staff see him as a helpful and capable leader? These questions cannot be answered accurately by administrators who have isolated themselves; they can only be answered with certainty if the supervisor has friendly and trusting relationships with the teachers and counselors he serves.

Recent research confirms what everyone suspects: persons with high self-esteem tend to be more optimistic and friendly; they are more accepting of themselves and others with whom they work (Hartman, 1964). Conversely, those who have low self-esteem tend to be more anxious, depressed, cynical and insecure about themselves and their relationships with others.

If one thinks of the human personality as being made up of parts which affect the behavior of the individual, then the job of coordinating and balancing them out becomes another function of the control structures (Blanck, 1974). The ego determines whether the demands of the impulsive system will be met or not; whether the requirements of the outside world or of concience will dictate how a person behaves. For instance, if the conscience of an administrator becomes the driving force behind his behavior toward others, he may feel that the right thing is being done even when it hurts others or denies some of the demands of his impulsive needs. But if he yields to his impulses, the supervisor may find himself coming into conflict with others who are offended by his conscienceless behavior. So the ego, or control structure, tries to keep a balance between these internal demands and the demands of the outside world.

A healthy ego seeks not only to know what is happening inside its mind and in the surrounding world, but also to make choices about what sorts of behavior would make the most sense. Since there are many ways to respond to different situations, the ego has a selection to make and this choice is based upon more than whether the individual can pay the social or moral price for his behavior. Let us asume that an assistant principal in an urban junior high school decides his principal's treatment of other administrators is sarcastic and unprofessional, but keeps silent because of fear of drawing the anger of his superior. Of course, he has a number of ways he can react to this situation. He can deny that the treatment really did humiliate and degrade the others. He can point to their lack of response and characterize it as proof they were not really offended. Then he will be annoyed with himself and anyone else who suggests that the behavior was sarcastic, overbearing and degrading and that someone should have said something. He may, as another reaction, simply withdraw by saying little at administrative meetings. Or he may decide that the other administrators 'had it coming to them', and avoid these people whenever possible; he may sit as far away from them as he can at meetings. He may decide to leave the school entirely, quietly asking for a transfer as soon as the opportunity presents itself. Or he may bring the principal's behavior to the attention of his superiors, accusing the principal of many violations and impropriety. Of course, he may decide to do none of these things, living with his feelings of inadequacy, guilt, anxiety and humiliation, suffering from the effects of these negative emotions.

This assistant principal has still more choices he can make. Maybe he can talk to the principal and ask him if he is aware of his behavior. Maybe he can ask an administrator who is closer to the chief to do this chore. Or maybe he can talk to others on the administrative staff, asking them for their suggestions for dealing with this problem. His ego will have these and many other choices to make.

A Lack of Control

An inability to control and harness libidinal or impulsive energy and drives and poor personal relationships with others appear to be linked together (Hartmann, 1964). In the school they can sometimes be symptomized by an 'I don't care', or an 'I don't need anyone or any help' attitude. For example the staff member may be shy or insecure and unable to enter into a relationship with fellow teachers and counselors. Administrative support systems do not deal with the past experiences and maladaptions which caused such behavior; rather they focus the attention of the member on how these feelings and behavior affect him now. They do not search out the past experiences which made such maladjustments necessary because such work is best done by a therapist. They do help teachers and counselors to become more aware of their patterns of behavior. ('You always get angry first and think afterward!') They do ask them to decide whether such adjustments and ways of responding to others are still fulfilling their old satisfactions. Staff members whose characteristic mode of behavior is one of anger may respond in the school setting by projecting their angry, unhappy feelings onto others with whom they work. This is often related to feelings that they are being judged or evaluated poorly by supervisors and other staff members. In these circumstances, supervisors should subordinate value judgments and criticisms in order to establish a good relationship; they should confront such persons in a gentle manner about the validity of their perceptions and understandings.

A special case which haunts many administrators (and teachers) is that of the paranoid slant. This pattern of thought is rooted in the feeling of supervisors that they cannot make a difference in their work and that this knowledge of their ineffectiveness is widely shared by other people in the school. When they adopt the paranoid slant, they find it necessary to shift the blame or guilt they feel (for being inadequate or inferior) to others with whom they work. ('If you people did your job, things wouldn't be so screwed up around here.') These feelings of ineffectiveness ('I guess I'm just a born loser') cause administrators and staff members to be careful in their associations with others since these may discover or confirm in their own minds evidence of their inferiority or inadequacy. If they are open and honest with others, these others will learn of their difficulties and use this knowledge against them. This feeling that others are plotting against them makes it more difficult for them to speak openly and has the unintended effect of moving people further away from them.

The tensions of the paranoid slant lead to an insight that it is not their actions or shortcomings but the behavior of those around them which are to blame for their ineffectiveness. By using the paranoid slant, they become the victim, not of their own inadequacies, but of the plotting and inefficiency of others. In this way, the guilt which they felt initially, although perhaps unconsciously, is no longer theirs. It has been transferred to those subordinates with whom they work. Administrators, teachers and counselors find it more difficult to know what is happening around them in this state of mind. They often repeat behaviors that antagonize others and cause them to become unfriendly and hostile. As for being sensitive to the ways in which they transfer blame to others, how they provoke others, or how they behave in ways in which are motivated by their impulsive energies and preconceptions — in these kinds of insights they are woefully inadequate. They find themselves unable to admit their mistakes and errors ('That would be giving them the ammunition they need!').

The breakdown of communication channels in schools, and the strain such failures can cause in all staff members and students in the building, often lead to an improper ego development in everyone concerned. They can cause ego regression, in which educators lose skills, abilities and understandings they had already mastered. This can happen when staff members are initiated into an authoritarian school environment which deemphasizes people, skills and problem solving methods.

Another related form of behavior is that of transference (Greenacre, 1959), which refers to the displacement of impulsive energies from one person to another. Usually the shift is from one's parents or early authority persons to individuals in the present. Thus, staff may show warmth and affection toward administrators when they first meet them. But after a period of time, other, more puzzling feelings and behavior may become evident. They, too, are associated with the kinds of relationships a teacher or counselor had with his or her parents. This means that staff may use this transference pheonomenon so they can react to new authority persons in ways which are characteristic of their personalities. They reactivate old attitudes and ways of responding so they will feel less anxious and afraid. They want to act toward the school leader as they did toward other powerful persons they knew in their past. Researchers have defined transference as a constellation of emotions which is energized by a compulsion to repeat the feelings and attitudes which belonged to past relationships by shifting or projecting them onto present day individuals. They interpret ongoing relationships in terms of their past associations and experiences. Greenacre, an important researcher in ego psychology, dealt with transference by focusing on the mother-child dyad, which she felt contained the core of the phenomenon. The attitude of the child toward the mother was developed in a relationship in which the child was essentially powerless and dependent for many years. The transference of these feelings onto administrators (or teachers and coumselors) can release a great deal of unneutralized aggression and drive energy; it can cause a great deal of distortion in the reception and understanding of communications between people working together in the school.

When supervisors try to use communication channels to change the way staff members react to them, they usually encounter resistance. These behaviors are the characteristic ways these teachers and counselors express themselves, and these behaviors are deeply rooted in their self-concepts and identities. So staff defend themselves against any efforts to innovate, at first; they look away from their own behavior and impulses.

They want to go on acting as they have done in the past. If they were friendly toward those who had power over them, they want to retain that way of reacting to present-day authority figures in their life. And, if they were angry and hostile, they have an interest in remaining that way. From this, administrators can see that their task is difficult: to deal with transference and resistance by accepting the staff member's stage of development; and to move him slowly from a lack of awareness of impulsive behavior toward a greater insight and control of these features of his personality. Certainly, there can be no change in the relationships between administrators and staff as long as this problem remains unresolved.

Ego Support

Ego support is an important tool of education administration (Redl and Wineman, 1952). It is more than merely encouraging or complimenting a staff member. 'That was good', 'you are well-liked', and so on are nothing more or less than flattery and mean little in a clinical, scientific sense. They make teachers and counselors feel good for the moment, but they also create feelings of anxiety and dependence upon the administrator. Will he feel that the next thing the teacher or counselor does is equally good? Or will he disapprove?

Anxiety and poor self-concepts cannot be affected by such compliments. The feelings a staff person has about himself were learned and internalized at an early age in relationships with parents and primary groups; they were affected also by his successes and failures in social and intellectual tasks. General compliments have little lasting effect upon persons who have a poor sense of themselves as individuals and professionals. And remember, even the best teacher or counselor lives in a society in which many believe that 'those that can, do; those who can't, teach'. So staff need more specific support if they are to properly appreciate their growth and development as faculty members and persons. Only then can they become aware of their own areas of increasing strength and competency. Only then can they be expected to use these new insights in their daily work with children. Initiative and a spirit of inquiry are fostered when ego functions are strengthened in this way. The courage to disagree and to try new things is another outcome of such practice.

But the opposite kinds of practices seem to be prevalent in today's schools. There seem to be a great deal of anxiety and defensiveness in relationships between staff and administrators. Staff tend to feel that administrators are untrustworthy and overly judgmental in their behavior and attitudes; administrators assume that teachers and counselors are lazy, apathetic and only interested in making more money. Staff feel they must submit to the directive leadership of incompetent supervisory personnel; administrators talk about disloyalty and pedagogical errors of teachers and counselors as they work with children in their classroom and offices.

An important problem for education is to find ways of improving this situation. One way is to establish greater empathy and regard between the two groups by strengthening the individual control structures of both staff and their supervisors. This is best done by encouraging faculty to verbalize their thoughts and feelings in regular supervisory meetings. Many staff are quiet and introspective because they fear ridicule or rejection. Some use this way of responding because they want the father-figure (administrators) to understand them without words, as their fathers and mothers did when they were infants. Of course, this is impossible. Still, school supervisors have to become friendly with these quiet ones, too; they need to learn about their inner feelings and thoughts; they need to encourage them to explain themselves in words. And they have to make sure they describe and interpret their experiences and feelings as they develop in schooling situations. The point to be remembered is that everyone has the capacity to self-disclose effectively. This is an important ego-building technique for both staff and their surpervisors. When staff verbalize their feelings and experiences, they set in motion a process that greatly strengthens the functioning of their control structures or egos (Jacobson, 1964). Verbalization forces them to substitute symbols for vague, remembered experiences; it makes them declare openly their intentions and reveals the way in which they see the school world within which they work. It helps staff to develop inner controls by assisting the control structures to neutralize urges and emotions emanating from the impulsive system. Some researchers have found that verbalization and neutralization help individuals to understand and tolerate frustration better in their everyday life (Rothstein, 1981).

So ego building is best done by encouraging teachers and counselors to complete consciousness; they know everything that is happening to them. Often, however, the conscious knowledge of events and relationships is buried in the subconscious. So it is best never to tell someone anything you want them to know. They know. And they can, usually, under skillful questioning, tell you their problems and concerns; they can draw conclusions from the information as easily as the supervisor can. At such moments, questions such as 'What does that mean to you?' or 'How would you interpret that?' can help staff to synthesize and evaluate their own behavior and feelings. Advice giving, which is so common in schools today, tends to intimidate teachers and counselors and to make them overly dependent and concerned with the judgments of their supervisors.

So verbalization within the framework of a friendly, trusting association is the key. It is the start of the neutralization or control process. Neutralization in supervisory meetings is strengthened primarily by verbalization which helps teachers and counselors to understand and cope with their emotions.

Example 1

'Today I met with a special education teacher. He was very nervous and upset as he sat in front of me. His hands moved constantly and his facial muscles were tighter than usual. This surprised me, since I assumed we were friends.

'Finally, he began to talk about his problem: one of his teachers in his department was an alcoholic; he was doing a poor job of teaching and he was hurting the children. Something had to be done about it. The other staff members and support staff wanted him to be their spokesman; they wanted him to lead them in an effort to have this man dismissed. But my friend insisted he wanted no part in such an action. He did not want to be pushed into a leadership role.

'We talked for a long time. My friend admitted that he didn't care for this alcoholic teacher. In fact, he remembered an incident in which this man had humiliated him in front of other staff members at a meeting. It happened soon after his appointment to the school. The alcoholic teacher accused him of being a weak, ineffective teacher who was causing problems for the rest of them. My friend remembered his feelings at the time: he felt a surge of anger and hatred toward his tormentor.

'Then my friend had an insight. He had sworn that day that he would get even with this man, but then put such thoughts out of his mind. Subconsciously, he plotted against the alcoholic teacher, talking with others about his drinking and inconsistent behavior. He wasn't being forced to be the leader in the struggle to rid the department of this man. He was the leader!

'This revelation startled the both of us. My friend was suprised at his devious behavior and the strength of his first feelings which he had apparently repressed. He decided to write up a plan for redressing the damage he had done to the alcoholic teacher. He had no desire to harm him any further and felt that he had to go out of his way make amends.

'Here was an instance where unconscious impulses and feelings distorted the perceptions of reality for my friend and caused behavior which he was unaware of until he verbalized his feelings and behavior to me in this session.'

Ego support requires that the work be done by teachers and counselors; the supervisor must not help them to do things they can do themselves. The supervisory conference encourages the staff member to focus on his problems in the classroom and guidance clinic. What are these difficulties? Who is involved in them? How is the teacher or counselor responding to the feelings and actions of other in these situations? These questions ask staff to become more involved in identifying and resolving their problems. It asks them to strengthen and use their own interpretive skills. This strengthens their ability to see, understand and respond consciously to the school world.

Verbalizing feelings acts as a substitute for actions which might hurt the teacher or counselor and his relationships in the school. At the very least it postpones overt behavior and causes the staff member to think about aspects of his situation which may have escaped his attention in the past. As one learns to transfer libidinal energies from the emotional to the more rational mode through the verbalization of feelings, one is better able to place these emotions and impulses under the control of the ego. The ego, in turn, becomes further strengthened and better able to rationalize the events which take place between them and the children they serve.

If supervisors cannot talk to staff members in this way, they do not have information or an opportunity to understand what is really happening in the school. They cannot act in conscious rational ways, or know how they are being understood and perceived by those with whom they work. They cannot know where their teachers or counselors are in their personal and professional development, and they cannot provide them with meaningful supervision and problem solving services.

Therefore, when a staff member cannot express himself, or when he is unaware of feelings, he feels anxiety, frustration and discomfort. The feelings, which are often related to actual school experiences, build up and force him to seek some way of relieving his growing inner tensions. If he does not express these feelings, or denies them, they tend to reappear at random times in irrational and unpleasant ways. If administrators, teachers and counselors do not deal with these feelings as they arise, they have to deal with a whole configuration of free-floating anger and anxiety later; and these feelings will seem to be detached from anything which will appear as irrational and unreasonable behavior. Telling oneself that these feelings don't exist, one may defend or prevent oneself from understanding the impulses and emotions for a while. But these patterns of behavior which are built on unconscious attitudes will keep slipping out in gestures, speech, voice tone and relationships with others. These problems are caused by one's inability to relate to one's own inner feelings and impulses and to those others with whom one works; and by one's general lack of sensitivity toward the kinds of emotional relationships one forms inside the school.

People have the capacity to like and dislike one another in the same moment, the same encounter (Jacobson, 1964). This makes it possible for them to associate and to carry on social intercourse. They often feel ambivalence between their needs and intentions, their ability to accept and reject features in the same situation or person. It is not known why people have these negative and positive reactions to one another; it is only known that they do and that these feelings are related to their need for love and acceptance. These same needs force people to hide their negative emotions, their feelings of hostility and anger. But the suppression or repression of feelings causes a new and more complicated emotion to appear: anxiety. Later Freudian thought held that tension and conflict between two psychic structures (ego and the id, as one example) produce anxiety and a need for the ego to institute defensive measures. The cycle, conflict-anxiety-defense, leads to symptom formations as a compromise between the two psychic structures. Together with anger, hostility and guilt, they form a configuration of defensive attitudes and behaviors which are often seen in schools today where love acceptance are often conspicuous by their absence.

Supervisors, too, need someone to talk to about their behavior and feelings. They need someone who can make them more aware of the moments when their anger shows itself in inappropriate unexpected ways. They must be able to see when they are upset, when they are taking over the work function from teachers and counselors, when they are demeaning or humiliating staff members by acting in provocative or hostile ways. Every supervisor and teacher or counselor must struggle with the ambivalent feelings which grow out of their work with people and their need to be the giving person in most of their school associations.

If, therefore staff do not have supervisors with whom they can talk about their hopes, dreams, fears and aspirations, they suffer a diminution of the spirit and social isolation. If they work in schools where they have no friends, and do not perceive administrators and fellow teachers and counselors as helpful persons, they suffer from feelings of exclusion and loneliness. If they are not permitted self-direction and a growing sense of achievement, their interest and involvement in their work decreases significantly. A teacher or counselor who has no one to talk to about his work cannot become sensitive to his needs and the needs of the children he is trying to serve.

Freedom from Traumatic Handling

An encounter between an administrator and staff person can be traumatic when it produces disturbed feelings and responses in either of them (Redl and Wineman, 1952). This is often because the experience reminds one of them of another past event or because it forces them to endure an attack on their self-esteem. A school administrator can cause a teacher or counselor to experience a traumatic episode when he touches upon matters which inflame past problems and difficulties or creates new ones; when he evokes anxiety, fear or defensiveness in the staff member. Whether a staff person will be traumatized by a supervisor's behavior depends on his previous life history and associations with other authority persons, and the nature of their relationship. It is generally conceded that teachers and counselors are often mistreated because of the reactive nature of administration in overcrowded, understaffed public schools. It is also known that staff members have the ability to withstand and overcome some measure of this traumatic handling; many of them take it in stride and manage to socialize their aggressive, hostile or embarrassed feelings. Still, administrators should, as much as possible, make certain that the staff are not humiliated or wrongly handled.

Two points should be emphasized. First, administrators should avoid angry, aggressive, unfriendly, judgmental confrontations which embarrass or show up staff members in front of others. Under no circumstances should they blame them in public. Releasing angry impulses is not acceptable behavior even when it makes the administrator 'feel better'; threats of any kind must be avoided and the consequences of competition dealt with in a warm and accepting manner. Situations which expose staff to ridicule, anxiety, fear or resentment must be eliminated. Favoritism and inconsistent treatment as well as tactlessness must also be avoided. Needless to say, these principles apply with greather force to the way teachers and counselors handle the defenseless, dependent children with whom they come in contact.

Second, along with this freedom from traumatic handling in the present, it is necessary for administrators to know something about the previous schooling and life experiences of staff members and students. It is necessary to know something of any previous wrong-handling they suffered in the past. The behavior of staff toward administration must be understood within the context of these past experiences and the feelings they are generating in the present. Aggressive or perverse behavior and impulses may be related to other times, places and persons. The question of whether a supervisor will give in to the demands of a teacher or counselor that a boy be permanently barred from class, or whether he will be asked to take the boy back 'one more time', must be made with some knowledge of a teacher's previous dealings with disruptive students. Supervisors must think about past situations in which the staff person was wrongly treated by administration and use this information to design a strategy which does not repeat past mistakes. This means that supervisors must have knowledge and skills in the areas of feelings, expression and inquiry. They must be aware of the normal responses and development of human personality in organizational settings.

Of course, all staff members and students go through experiences in schools which have some traumatic impact. Everyday school life is impersonal. Mass schools cannot be so insulated and controlled that individuals are protected from these humiliating occurrences. The youngster who has been humiliated in front of his classmates and has feelings of shame and embarrassment has been traumatized. Of course the level of trauma is not as great as that which is associated with the death of a parent or serious personal injuries. Even so, the trauma of living and working in unfriendly and unsupportive classrooms and guidance centers can have a stunning effect on a child's personality and intellectual development. Seldom do teachers and counselors recognize the symptoms of this kind of trauma; passivity can actually go unnoticed (or praised) in many schools and classrooms today. With competition the rule, one can make a generalization: the grading of deportment and work in a competitive ethos can be seen as a traumatic handling of children, especially when it happens in kindergarten and first grade.

Example 2
Sabra, who had spent four months in a kindergarten class in a suburban school, was becoming withdrawn and uninterested in schoolwork. She told of doing simple tasks she had done when she was much younger. Her mother asked for more information and was told that Sabra was in the green group in her class. When pressed further, Sabra said that was the smart group and that another group, the 'yellows' as they were called, were for the dummies. Here was tracking of children in kindergarten! When Sabra's mother spoke to the teacher, she confirmed what Sabra had told her. The children in the yellow group were mostly from the nearby military base and much slower than the neighborhood children. 'Do you know,' the teacher said, 'those children don't even know their colors! They don't even know that they have a last name!'

The injuriousness to the self-concepts of children in this situation is self-evident, but the teacher seems to be unaware of it. Unsupportive, cold contact with teachers or counselors who feel they are incompetent and unworthy persons certainly causes trauma in the children. For the trauma is inherent in the handling of these 'dummies' both by teachers and by the children in the class.

The commitment to provide administrative support systems begins with a specific problem: how to restructure the schooling organization so as to improve the communication patterns between staff members and administrators. It ends with the development of a cultural system which is at variance with traditional educational practice; which seeks to improve the quality of life for staff members and the students they serve.

The benefits of such a support system are many sided:

they help teachers and counselors to understand the emotional and behavioral consequences of many of their actions;

they help staff members to understand their own behavior and their contributions to situations of stress and conflict;

they help teachers and counselors to see that there are many different ways to do their work;

they help staff members to learn how they process information and what distortions they are prone to as a result of their own unique social and psychological histories;

they help teachers and counselors to gain an increased measure of empathy for their students and to learn to see the world through the eyes of others;

they help staff members to accept all kinds of behavior as normal and meaningful;

they help teachers and counselors to be more flexible in their use of authority so they can limit the frustration and anxiety of the children with whom they work;

they help staff to use inquiry methods to learn about the problems of children;

they encourage others to develop their own ways of solving problems.

In these ways the school is made more responsive to the needs of its members. Supervisors work through their staff members; they do not take over the work function in 'order to show how it should be done'. They assume the role of the facilitator, inquirer and friend.

Ego support systems are preeminently face-to-face engagements in which the supervisor, because of training and insight with respect to his own behavior, the behavior of others and the effects of certain situations on people, helps staff to work in more conscious, effective ways.

Key Points

1 Providing a supportive environment for teachers creates the necessary climate for proactive decision making.
2 A proactive principal's most critical information source is his faculty. He must be aware of their needs and prepared to respond when necessary.
3 An effective principal must have a grounding in psychology in order to work, counsel, support and guide his faculty and staff.
4 The 'feelings' of people must be articulated and addressed in order for legitimate communication to exist. A proactive principal is aware of this and attempts to create an environment for this to occur.

Discussion Questions

1 From a socio-psychological point of view, what does Rothstein cite as important proactive leadership traits?
2 How should a proactive principal define individual and staff identity? How can this perception be utilized in proactive desision making?
3 What are the benefits Rothstein articulates regarding communication and self-disclosure?
4 How does a proactive decision maker build 'ego' in his faculty?
5 How would you define 'information sources' in the context of Rothstein's analysis?

References

BLANCK, G.R. (1974) *Ego Psychology: Theory and Practice*, New York, Columbia University Press, pp. 344–6.

GREENACRE, P. (1959) 'Certain technical problems in the transference relationship', *Journal of the American Psychoanalytic Association*, 7, pp. 484–502.

HARTMANN, H. (1964) *Essays in Ego Psychology*, New York, International Universities Press, pp. 81–2.

JACOBSON, E. (1964) *The Self and the Object World*, New York, International Universities Press (see also the works of Heinz Hartmann, Anna Freud and E. Kris).

REDL, F. and WINEMAN, D. (1952) *The Aggressive Child*, Glencoe, Free Press, pp. 29–44; see also ROTHSTEIN, S.W. (1975) 'Conflict resolution in a supportive environment', *Education and Urban Society*, February, pp. 193–206.

ROTHSTEIN, S.W. (1981) 'The focus overview', *The Guidance Clinic*, December, pp. 1–6; see also ROTHSTEIN, S.W. (1984) 'Ego support in a supportive environment', *The Guidance Clinic*, February.

ROTHSTEIN, S.W. (1983) 'The socialization of the school administrator', *Private School Quarterly*, Spring, pp. 52–60.

ROTHSTEIN, S.W. (in preparation) *Anxiety and Defensiveness in Staff-Administrative Relationships*.

Section Four: Interactive Video Simulations: An Innovative Approach to Develop Decision-Making Skills
Andrew E. Dubin

The use of interactive video is an exciting and innovative curriculum approach to studying and developing decision-making abilities in students pursuing leadership positions in our public schools. Although effective decision making is the cornerstone of any efficient organization, finding and developing effective methods of teaching this important skill is highly elusive. It is virtually impossible to identify all of the organizational, psychological, sociological, political and economic factors that underscore a single decision so as to develop a single cogent theory or framework. Decisions require something of a frame-by-frame perusal in order to promote intelligent understanding and analysis. An effective decision-making pedagogy must be flexible enough to include a variety of factors that may impinge on a decision-making situation, yet focused enough to provide direction and clarity in developing systematic guidelines students can use to make sound decisions.

Interactive video is a new application of technology that helps develop the requisite skills necessary to analyze and make sound decisions. It is particularly effective in developing decision-making abilities for it marries theory and practice, integrating the practical reality of an actual case study with a sound theoretical framework. This 'connection' is proving to be a highly effective way to socialize graduate students in educational administration to the importance of sound decision making. In fact, the process of socialization itself, the role development or status position training that designates the specific behaviors, abilities, beliefs, values, emotional dispositions and norms appropriate in a particular social setting and structure, is crucial in all training institutions (Becker and Casper, 1956). By using actual case studies, interactive video is able to capture a real-life 'social setting and structure', freeze-frame it, and allow viewers to analyze the practical and theoretical aspects of the case. Its use within a secure, unfettered academic arena generates thoughtful reflection. Its realistic school-site setting and enactment, along with the response required of the viewer, provides the closest thing to an actual decision-making situation in a school. I shall illustrate how such an interactive video case study can be developed, but let us look first at some other pedagogical approaches that focus on the use of decision-making technology and examine cognitive processes involved in making decisions.

Most computerized decision-making programs dealing with school problems or issues are generally linear in nature, in that the program is written in print form and calls for a rationally-based response. The work of John Hunt, for example, focuses on an interactive computer mimetic 'game'. This program calls upon a group of three individuals to analyze a problem. An administrator and two teachers, one of whom had extensive experience and one who had little experience, were placed in front of a computer and asked a series of questions that called for specific decisions.

> The computer mimetic game placed each group, working alone, into the principalship of an elementary school with the assignment to expend the resources provided so as to improve fourth

grade achievement scores. The decision group was introduced within the 'game' to data about the school, the teachers, the students and the community; and taught how to 'thumb' the information as and whenever the group wished. In addition, the decision group was provided within the computer the effective schools research to which had been attached decision pathways and sub-pathways; each of which had a benefit potential for improving the fourth grade scores and a cost potential in staff time and/or allocated dollars. The actions of each decision group were recorded within the computer and each decision group was observed. (Hunt, 1989)

Although the results were of interest as to the ways by which groups developed cohesiveness, focus and decision-making skills, a further finding was that a group's ability to make effective decisions was directly correlated to its working together as a decision-making team, and that these abilities were applicable only to that given situation, that is, only in the context of a laboratory setting. In order for these skills to be transferred to a real-life site, the group must be transplanted to the actual site environment so that they can work together to more accurately measure their decision-making capabilities. The key finding that emerged from Hunt's work was that the longer the group worked together in the lab setting, the more able they were in making effective decisions.

Coleman (1973) and others have identified certain basic differences between what they call 'Experiential Learning' and 'Information-Processing Learning'. The steps in Information-Processing Learning are:

reception of information (through a symbolic medium);

understanding the general principal (assimilation of this information as knowledge);

particularizing (inferring a particular application from the general principle);

acting (use of information received).

The steps in Experiential Learning are:

acting (acting in a particular instance);

understanding the particular case (understanding the effects or consequences in the particular instance);

generalizing (understanding the general principle under which the particular case falls);

application (application through action in a new circumstance with the range of the generalization).

The focus of Coleman's work was to draw distinctions between the processes of learning and what impact games have on that process. An interesting aspect of his analysis appears when it is compared to neurological research which focuses on hemispheric functions of the brain. Some studies which identify brain function location have shown that 'right hemispheric (appositional) thought is non-verbal, non-linear, perceptual, musical, holistic, integrative, in three-dimensional space but non-dimensional time, whereas left hemispheric (propositional) thought is verbal, linear, conceptual, non-musical and fragmented' (Coleman, 1976). With distinctions of brain function in mind, simulations could have a particularly strong impact on the learner. The integration of interactive video with the linear component included within the simulation (linear programming), requires the viewer to respond on several levels. The viewer is being asked to rationalize the situation within an emotionally charged environment requiring a complex series of reactions. The constant by-play of decision, decision-option and consequence triggers a dialectic process that requires the integration of distinct functions of the brain. 'This concept can be extended to viewing propositional thought as reasoning through division or partition of phenomena (including time), and oppositional thought as focusing on reasoning through integration and consideration of the totality of phenomena (including time)' (Bogen, 1969). Thus, interactive video, from the standpoint of its impact on brain function, could be an effective methodology to dissect, analyze and synthesize different types of complex information.

Feurstein (1976) and others investigated the relationship between cognition and 'mapping', that is, the ways by which a learner internalizes, organizes and experiences information. They analyzed the cognitive process of learning by breaking down the component parts involved into seven areas:

a mental act;

modality or language used for communication;

phase of cognition function required;

cognitive operations required (analyses, comparisons);

levels of abstraction, complexity (how many items to integrate, analyze-cognitive functions, discrete processes and new skills);

levels of abstraction-concrete art and application;

levels of efficiency, speed, accuracy and perceived effort.

Within this cognitive construct of learning, they further analyzed the cognitive functions involved in the thinking process: input — the gathering of information; elaboration — the processing or using of information; and output — the expressing of a solution. In the *input* phases, Feurstein focuses on the identification of the information, labelling it and essentially giving it some parameters based upon the specific learner receiving the information. In the *elaboration* phase, a closer assessment of the information is undertaken by the learner underscored by his/her ability to make comparisons, relationships, categorizations, pictures, in order to comfortably place that information in his/her mind. Lastly, the *output* phase is the expression of the information through effective strategies.

Sinatra and others have focused on another aspect of 'mapping' as it applies to reading. He found that a 'semantic map or network is a graphic arrangement showing how the major and minor ideas are related in a written work' (Sinatra *et al.*, 1986) (see Figure 4.4). While this research emphasizes mapping as applied to reading and understanding, the process of information organizing relates well to interactive video utilization. One specific type of map is called a 'Thematic or Descriptive Map', in which the map 'displays elements and details about persons, places or things around the central theme. Associated relationships are portrayed as stemming from the main concept' (*ibid.*). The associative feature in this map defines information as tangential yet directed and connected to the principal feature of the theme or main idea or, in the context of decision making, is known as a decision option. In an interactive video presentation, a menu display visualizes the various 'mapping' alternatives that are available to the viewer in a way similar to a reading 'map'.

Ohlhausen and Roller (1988) focused on 'schema theory' as another way of analyzing how information is processed. Schema theory suggests that we use text structure and content schemata to help us select important information. In short, as a reader processes information in a text, it is utilized in specific ways in order to understand and internalize it. One aspect of the analysis involves the reader's understanding the author's style and approach; the other deals with the reader's personal perception assumed to analyze the material. In a similar way, a decision option undertaken depends upon the context of the situation as well the cultural bias of the decision maker. Again, although this refers specifically to reading applications, the transference of applications is clear.

Sweeney and Beyer's work on adult learning and critical thinking offers some further insights regarding the ways in which adults process information. Focusing on the adult learner, they delineate learning principles and the respective implications for course design. This research suggests an effective pedagogy should feature an interactive mode which viscerally engages the learner. Since the adult learner comprises the majority of administrative candidates in graduate school, the use of interactive video as a teaching tool offers a viable means to address their learning needs.

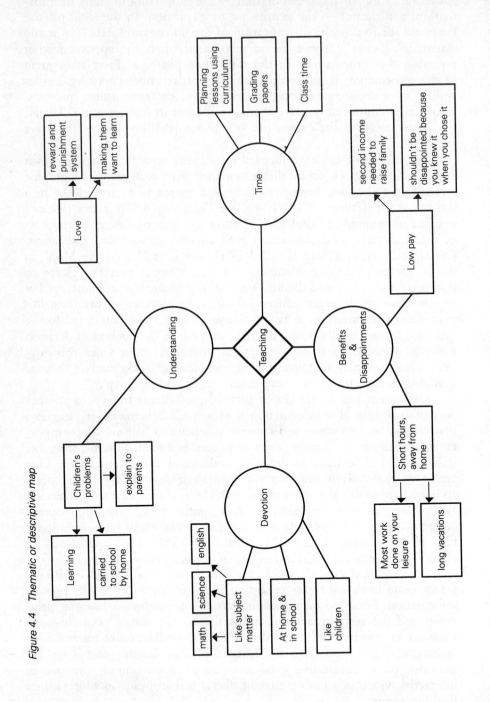

Figure 4.4 Thematic or descriptive map

Learning Principles	*Implications/Course Design*
The adult is a partner with the instructor in the learning process.	Participants should actively influence the learning approach.
Adults are capable of taking the responsibility for their own learning.	Incorporate self-direction into course learning design.
Adult learners gain through two-way communication.	Avoid use of lectures and 'talking-to'; emphasize discussion.
Adults learn through reflection on their own and others' experience.	Use interactive methods such as case studies, role playing, etc.
Adults learn what they perceive to be useful in their own lives.	Make the content closely aligned with assessed needs.
Adults' attention spans are a function of their interest and activities.	Allow plenty of time to process the learning experience.
Adults are most receptive to instruction that is clearly related to problems they face daily.	Include applications planning in each learning activity.
Adults learn best when they are treated with respect.	Promote inquiry and affirm the experience of participants.
Adults filter their learning through their value systems.	Provide activities that focus on cognitive, affective and behavioral change.

The Use of Interactive Video

Interactive video is the integration of a video simulation onto a computerized program. After a case study is conceptualized, developed, simulated and taped, it is transferred, that is, programmed onto a computer disc. In this state, the viewer can see the case study on the computer monitor and respond to a series of options and consequences that are presented. With the use of the IBM InfoWindow Touch Screen, the viewer is able to literally touch the monitor when information is presented in order to trigger the programmed response selected.

How can a case study be developed so that the decision-making process is analyzed? How can the human variable, which underscores each case study, be programmed so that there are finite possibilities or 'boundary conditions' (Drucker, 1966)? How many consequences or decision options are there that result from the initial decisions taken? Is there a final decision and how does the overall process compare to decision-making models in the literature? Does this pedagogy reflect a more advanced or effective method for general instruction or specifically decision making? These are just a sampling of the questions and points of analysis required in the conceptualization and development of an interactive video case study.

When the late George Hallowitz and I first developed the use of a case study involving the application of decision making through the use of interactive video, we studied hundreds of decisions made by principals in K-12 settings. We examined the most commonly used locations, topics and personnel involved in those decisions. We considered the various options that were generated as a result of those decisions. We reflected on the role descriptions ascribed to all the players in each case study by each principal in order to understand their responses.

Analysis of the case studies reveals that principals are involved in decisions every few minutes. They are most often responsive and reactive, rather than deliberate and proactive in their decision making (Dubin and Hallowitz, 1989). These decisions take place in a number of site locations, for example, the principal's office, general office, cafeteria, staff room, library, gymnasium, auditorium, a teacher's classroom, a counselor's office, other administrative office, the supply room, playing fields, parking lot, and so forth. Essentially, wherever the principal roams he/she is usually making some kind of a decision. As a general rule, though, most decisions that involve other faculty input are initiated in a more formalized setting, in either a staff, department or general council meeting. At these times, school personnel (assistant principals, counselors, department heads) offer information concerning the school about which the principal should be alerted. Although the context can be viewed as a rational one in that information is being presented in a logical, sequential manner, rather than a fragmented 'on-the-run' format, it nonetheless triggers off a series of complex responses (both rational and non-rational) on the part of the principal. At that time, the principal must begin to process that information about the problem. What should the decision-making process involve? What should be done first? In effect, the principal begins an internal conversation with himself. This dialectic triggers off the option-consequence sequence pathway of decision making addressed in the interactive video presentation.

An Example of a Case Study: Sexual Abuse

It is important to remember that decision making requires that the administrator have a sufficient amount of time to follow through with all the prescribed steps in order to reach a decision that is underscored by a grasp of their consequences. Each part of the decision-making process is quite important because it provides the foundation for the next sequence of decisions. When an emotional component enters into the equation (easily identified in the visual scenario because of the reaction of the players), the logic of the decision becomes highly personalized. The initial decision-making formula is, thus, altered in some way. This insight demands that decision makers be aware and in control of the emotional component involved in process. It also initiates, by way of selective perception, the special lenses through which the decision will be made.

The following interactive video case study centers around a principal's cabinet meeting in a senior high school. The cabinet includes an assistant principal, a counselor, a department chair and the principal, all of whom are sitting around the principal's conference table discussing various school related issues. The meeting takes place every Monday and either emphasizes important school events, identifies personnel matters, or discusses community activities, student concerns and/or projects. Agenda items are developed by the principal with input from the council.

The situation to be discussed was brought to the attention of the council by the counselor. She stated that she was informed that a student was being sexually harassed by one of the teachers. Her impression (based on an emotionally charged phone call she received from the student's parent and minister), was that the student interpreted certain remarks made in class by the teacher as being sexually suggestive. The student was extremely upset by these remarks and informed her parents and the family minister. They, in turn, contacted the counselor, and she was now bringing it to the attention of the principal for analysis and action. In addition to the information being conveyed to the principal, an emotional attachment is also being communicated by the way in which the counselor is transmitting the facts and the ways in which the other cabinet members are responding to the information. All of this information flow is affecting the principal and impacts on his/her first decisions.

At this juncture of the interactive video, a series of decision options are offered. What are the alternative information gathering options available to the principal and in what order should they be pursued? Should these options be communicated to the other cabinet members? Exactly what input should be solicited from the cabinet members, if any, and at what time? These are some of the questions that are generated by the interactive presentation.

At this point in the video, the viewer is presented with a 'menu',

Figure 4.5   Decision options 1

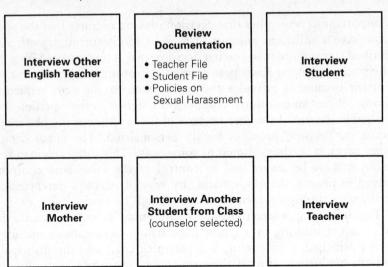

a graphic display that offers several options or decision choices. These options reflect the alternatives open to the principal to explore in order to come up with a decision. The menu then displays various options from which the viewer is asked to make a selection. The touch screen feature of the monitor enables the viewer to immediately summon forward a re-enacted consequence of each specific decision. It provides the viewer with the immediate feedback as to the impact of that information. The instant gratification of this process is particularly effective because of the speed of the response. After that particular consequence is examined, the viewer can proceed back to the menu and select another option, touch the screen and summon forward the re-enacted consequence of that decision. Again, after viewing that interaction, a decision is made as to whether the viewer feels unable to make a final decision.

Several decision options are generated by the initial information presented at the cabinet meeting to the Principal by the counselor (see Figure 4.5). One option is to review the teacher's evaluation and teaching history. Had there been any incidents in the teacher's past of a similar nature? Reflected in the literature on organizational process, teacher evaluations are generally conducted by subordinates, that is assistant principals and vice principals, rather than the principal himself although he/she should be cognizant of all evaluations. They, in turn, make appropriate recommendations to the principal regarding that evaluative process which initiates the principal's overall review of that teacher. Therefore, the decision option for the principal to review the record of the teacher in question is a viable and extremely important information source.

Another decision option is to interview the teacher to get his/her perspective. It is extremely important for the principal to be directly informed by the teacher in question. A critically important aspect to this option is the way in which the interview is conducted. If the principal approaches the teacher from an accusatory point of view, the interview will likely result in a negative exchange and be counterproductive to obtaining accurate information. That is one reason why each decision taken by the principal must possess both an understanding of the information presented, as well as a sense of his/her own bias and/or 'gut feeling' with respect to the situation and how it should be approached.

Another decision option is to interview the student in question. Again, finding out about the information directly from those who are affected is the only sure way to ascertain the specifics of the matter. In addition, interviewing the student communicates to the student (and ultimately the student body and parents) the principal's willingness to obtain all points of view. What specifically did this student hear the teacher say in class? In what context was it said ? These and other probing questions could asked in a non-judgmental, non-threatening way.

A further decision option is to interview another student in the class. In this way comparative data can be collected and used in the principal's analysis. This option would involve a close review of the specific student whose feedback is sought. What is the student's background regarding the subject matter? What is the student's relationship with the teacher and/or the other student?

Yet another option is to interview a colleague of the teacher who teaches in the same department. In this way comparative data could be collected and used in the analysis. How does this teacher's methodology or readings compare to the teacher in question? What is the general feeling expressed by the colleague about the teacher? The nature of the interview, that is, the way in which the meeting is conducted by the principal, of course, is extremely important.

A parent conference is another decision option. In this case, the parent was concerned by the child's reaction to the class interaction and required an audience with the principal. In this conference the parent could communicate information and receive some. Initially, the need for the parent to ventilate is an important administrative strategy. Of course, what the parent heard from the student will likely be more personalized. Whatever attitude the parent assumes during this conference must be mediated by the principal. Counsel, not confrontation, is what is necessary.

Each decision option triggers off a decision consequence, that is, the re-enactment of that particular decision option. What results from the decision consequence in terms of the next tier pursuit of that option can not be fully realized, of course, until the situation is viewed. As indicated, the perceived outcomes from each option will affect the decision-making process and the follow-up decision options. It is important to note that,

Figure 4.6   Decision options 2

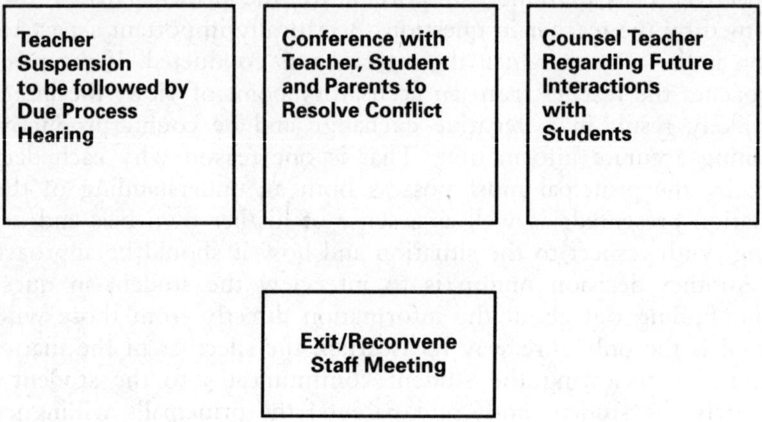

Teacher Suspension to be followed by Due Process Hearing	**Conference with Teacher, Student and Parents to Resolve Conflict**	**Counsel Teacher Regarding Future Interactions with Students**

Exit/Reconvene Staff Meeting

although various options have been advanced as viable alternatives, the principal may feel competent to make a decision early on. For example, after interviewing the teacher, student and parent, the principal may feel competent to make a decision. From the standpoint of this exercise, let us assume that the principal explored all the decision options offered in the menu, one at a time, and based upon the analysis of each consequence, decided to explore the second round of decision options and the information provided with them.

In the present example, the next series of decision options are limited to three (see Figure 4.6). The principal can choose to counsel the teacher. The potential outcome consequences of that interaction might be (and again, dependent upon the skill of the administrator and the relationship with the teacher) either reconciliation or confrontation. The teacher could be more sympathetic, flexible and willing to negotiate with the principal or could contest the entire matter, feeling harassed, victimized, or possibly slandered. All are potential outcome consequences. Another decision option could be to schedule a conference among the teacher, parent, student and principal. In this way all the views would be clearly articulated. How effective this interaction would be is again dependent upon the facilitative skill of the principal and the emotional attachment each person has to a particular outcome.

Following the second tier of option-consequence viewing, the interactive video returns to the next weekly council meeting where the executive faculty awaits the principal's decision. They indicate that the school is aware of the problem and that an immediate decision is expected. At this time, the viewer has either to make decision based on the information that has been reviewed, proceed along a different tack in collecting data or stall the decision. The case scenario ends at this point.

Student Reactions

Administrative candidates who have viewed the interactive video simulation described above found the case presentation highly stimulating and thought-provoking. Initially, they were asked to respond to a pre-test which asked them whether they had experienced the use of interactive video prior to that class session. Must students (n = 28) had not heard of interactive video, let alone experienced its use. They were also asked whether they felt case study analyses in general were helpful in developing decision-making skills. They all felt that such analyses were extremely useful, informative and instructive in developing such skills.

After viewing the interactive video, all administrative students felt that the material presented and the way in which it was experienced was highly effective in encouraging analytical thinking, free exchange within the small group arrangements, and in creating a realistic setting that allowed for exploration and assessment of alternative. In addition, the option-consequence was very well received, they said, because it offered an opportunity to assess a number of immediate and likely outcomes. It also helped them identify information sources to probe in order to make more reasonable decisions.

The development of this unique application of video simulations with the IBM InfoWindow Touch Screen computer required assistance from experts in educational technology as well as educational administration. Students in our Educational Technology Program (cited on the video case study) as well as the faculty from that department played a significant role in the development of these materials. Indeed, the merging of these two fields, technology and education, is a major breakthrough in the delivery system for training/educating teachers and administrators in our public schools today.

Conclusion

Interactive video offers an innovative and highly effective pedagogy in developing more advanced critical thinking abilities. It is the most sophisticated and still practical method through which the academic environment of the university setting can link with the 'real world' environment of our public schools. The potential for its application is, quite obviously, enormous ranging from the context of analytical decision making for aspiring administrators, to critical thinking skills in children.

Key Points

1 Interactive video is an extremely effective pedagogy that directly involves administration candidates in the decision-making process.

2 Cognitive mapping underscores decision-making processes and is a part of the interactive format.
3 Interactive video allows for shared decision making since it allows administrative candidates an opportunity to share their decisions as a group.
4 A dynamic feature of interactive video is that the consequences of the decision-making options available to administration candidates as they examine a case study can be immediately reviewed on the computer monitor.

Discussion Questions

1 What advantages are there in utilizing interactive video in the development of leadership skills for aspiring administrators?
2 Do you find the process of 'cognitive mapping' in analyzing decisions important for administrators and proactive decision makers? Please explain.
3 Please relate your exposure to this application of case study simulations and computer programming.
4 Is the case study discussed in the above section reflective of a situation you have experienced in your teaching/administrative background?
5 In your opinion, in what other ways can interactive video be utilized in order to develop skills in teachers, students, etc.?

References

BECKER, H. and CASPER, J.W. (1956) 'The development of identification with an occupation', *American Journal of Sociology*, 61, pp. 289–97.
BOGEN, J.F. (1969) 'The other side of the brain: Dysgraphia and dystopia following cerebral commissurotomy', *Bulletin of the Los Angeles Neurological Societies*, p. 34.
COLEMAN, J. *et al.* (1973) 'The Hopkins Games Program: Conclusions from seven years of research'. *Educational Researcher*, Vol. 2.
DUBIN, A. and HALLOWITZ, G. (1989) 'Research into decision making: A pilot project', *School of Education Review*, 1, 1, Spring, pp. 28–33.
DRUCKER, P. (1966) *The Effective Executive*, New York, Harper & Row.
FEURSTEIN, R. (1976) *Hadassah*, Wizo-Canada-Research Institute.
GRIFFITHS, D. (1959) *Administrative Theory*, New York, Appleton-Century-Crofts, Inc.
HUNT, J. (1989) 'Incipient studies of school-based decision groups', paper delivered at the conference, Emerging Technologies in Education and Training: A Bridge to Tomorrow, Augusta, Maine.
LYNCH, J. (1976) 'Neurological research and a theory of learning in

games: Are we asking the correct questions about the value of simulations?', unpublished manuscript.

MEYER, B.J.F. (1975) 'Identification of the structure of prose and its implications for the study of reading and memory', *The Journal of Reading Behavior*, 7, pp. 7–47.

OHLHAUSEN, L. and ROLLER, B. (1988) 'The operation of text structure and content schemata in isolation and in interaction', *Reading Research Quarterly*, 23, 1, pp. 71–88.

SINATRA, R., STAHL-GEMAKE, J. and MORGAN, N.W. (1986) 'Using semantic mapping after reading to organize and write original discourse', *Journal of Reading*, October, pp. 4–13.

SWEENEY, C. and BEYER, B. (1989) *The influence of Adult Learning, Critical Thinking and Cooperative Learning Strategies in University Classrooms*, The International Society for Exploring Teaching Alternatives, Ft.Collins.

TAYLOR, B.M. (1980) 'Children's memory for expository text after reading', *Reading Research Quarterly*, 15, pp. 399–411.

Chapter 5

Proactive Decision Making in Action: Experiences from Exemplary Teachers

Introduction

Principals who practice proactive decision making make a strong impact on their faculty and staff. Specifically, what are the feelings of the teachers impacted by these effective leaders? To what extent do these teachers feel more committed to their professional roles in the schooling process based upon their principal's leadership style? And, most importantly, what do they perceive the principals do in generating these positive and constructive attitudes in their teachers? These were some of the areas of interest and articulation in the following comments from award winning teachers.

Teachers feel very strongly that principals must know their faculty and school needs well in order to provide ample opportunity for them to develop professionally and for the school to progress successfully. For example, if the principal understands the curriculum and the faculty expertise, he will create appropriate staff development opportunities in order to prepare them to work with that curriculum more effectively. In another instance, if the principal desires greater shared decision making which would involve more faculty in that process, he will provide opportunities where teachers can experience situations where that skill can be developed.

Lastly, whether the principal is involved with community relations, or directing the school program, or being the 'change agent', he always assumes the proactive position through modeling. Effective proactive leadership is evidenced through action and behavior. Successful, vital teachers desire principals who are competent, have strong belief systems and demonstrate this high level professional performance.

Andrew E. Dubin

Jeannette Y. Grogan
*MA, Bilingual Education, Bilingual Kindergarten Teacher, Downer
Whole Language School, Richmond Unified School District, RUSD
Teacher-of-the-year, 1987*

As a classroom teacher, I work in an environment isolated from other adults. My main interaction with peers and administrators usually occurs outside the classroom setting. Since I view my professionalism as a continuing refinement of my classroom methodologies, I am concerned about how to obtain the information and feedback needed for improvement.

In considering the goal of how to foster professional development in myself and in my peers. I believe the principal plays a central role. The principal sets the professional tone of the school by applying his own expertise in curriculum and management. It is my experience that a principal must provide teachers with the incentive and vehicles not only to bring them out of their isolation, but also to encourage their professional interaction. That is, he must provide staff with a variety of options through which they can develop, share and extend their expertise. For the incentives to be real and the vehicles to work, the principal must have the information necessary to know the staff well in order to genuinely respect and channel their skills. Furthermore, he must display this informed confidence in his staff by listening to teachers' ideas, making appropriate suggestions and facilitating the transfer of information.

Moreover, the principal must value research and its implications for practice if he is to successfully guide a coherent schoolwide curriculum. This coherency can be achieved by the principal suggesting partnerships and informal mentorships based on his knowledge of who has what information and/or skills to share. He should also formalize this interaction by establishing professional study groups to seek out resources, to share information and to plan school/classroom programs based on this information. None of these actions I have mentioned would be effective without the existence of a work environment/dynamic that is conducive and supportive of change. We, as teachers, must feel that it is acceptable to take risks and suffer the small defeats and setbacks necessary for information.

I believe that this validation of the change process is best delivered during yearly teacher evaluations. The first meeting of the process must be more than a rubber stamp session. It must be truly reciprocal with the teacher stating his or her goals and the principal working with the teacher to refine them, hopefully ensuring their success. During the observation phase, the principal, while keeping in mind the goals, must clearly display his or her support and understanding of the challenges the practitioner faces while taking the risks necessary for improvement.

182

Most importantly, the principal must be capable of providing sensitive, informed feedback that increases the teacher's confidence and gives him or her concrete, logical, next steps.

Since I feel the key to my professionalism is the continual redefining and reshaping of my curriculum to best meet my students' needs. I want to work with a principal who encourages professional interaction, facilitates the exchange of information, validates and channels his teachers' skills and thereby creates the environment essential to the provision of a high quality school program.

Grita Z. Kamin
Master Teacher, First Grade, Downer Whole Language School,
Richmond Unified School District, Recipient, Richmond Education
Fund Grant

I have been a primary teacher in inner-city schools for twenty years, and a union activist throughout. When asked to define the role of a principal I would invariably knee-jerk to an adversarial response. But for two of those twenty years I had a principal whose excellence forced me to reexamine my assumptions. What differentiated this principal from his predecessors was, first and foremost, he was an educator and not a bureaucrat. He used his new administrative role to extend the lessons he had learned as an effective classroom teacher and to apply them in the context of a larger community.

Just as an effective teacher implies a well-managed classroom with an engaged group of participating students, all actively involved in learning, so an effective principal implies that a school's program is firmly established and that its philosophy and goals are understood and affirmed by the community it serves. This achievement requires a principal who:

has an excellent knowledge of curriculum and theory;

understands and respects the community he works in and utilizes its strengths to enhance the school program;

sets high expectations for himself, for the staff, for the students and for the parents;

is an articulate, courageous defender of innovation;

is viable and accessible to students, staff and parents;

is an advocate for his staff and community when dealing with other administrators and the public at large;

actively participates in the training of inexperienced or ineffective teachers;

engages outside agencies for help in dealing with the social, economic and medical problems which may beset the school community;

is a fair and consistent disciplinarian.

While this list in no way exhausts the requirements for an effective
principal, it highlights the essential qualities and activities that drive all
effective principals. It redefines the role of the principal not as an authoritarian, but a teacher and participator with the staff, and larger community. Just as a classroom teacher must understand the needs of his or her
students, and the strengths they bring with them, so a principal must
know and understand the staff's needs and strengths and those of the
community they serve.

Emily T. Vogler
*Master Teacher, Third Grade, Downer Whole Language School,
Richmond Unified School District, Recipient of Richmond Education
Fund Grants and State CTIPP Grant*

Originally, I undertook this discussion of effective principals believing a
few words would suffice. It grew in complexity as I realized I wanted
much more in a principal than any one person could give.

Ineffective principals cannot motivate teachers to be at their best.
They cannot impart to the students that desire to be one of the best, or
at least all they can be. A school without effective leadership will lack
community spirit and a unified sense of purpose. Worst of all, an in
effective principal will often lose his or her best teachers.

Today, all teachers and principals are under close public scrutiny. We
are encountering a rising public demand for thorough information on the
quality of our schools. There is a cry for vouchers. The public pressure
for greater assessment of teachers and students and calls for more accountability put new and increasing pressures on educators. These new pressures often put teachers and administrators in adversarial roles. In the face
of these pressures, the principal I work under has encouraged a strong,
cooperative sense of who we are as a staff and where we want to go as a
school. He has respected each teacher's unique style, but nurtured the
essential traits necessary to every school climate: enthusiasm, creativity
and caring.

To meet these public demands and achieve a professional and col-
legial climate, the principal must set the highest goals possible for his
school and staff. In order to set high goals, a principal must believe in
the abilities of his students and appreciate the richness of their cultural
diversity. In turn, he must also appreciate, encourage and set the stage for
the success of the staff's attempts to meet these students' needs and
enhance their lives.

Of the numerous qualities that go into making an effective principal, the one I find most important is a sense of imagination and the intelligence, creativity and sense of humor that issue from it. My best principals have been great teachers first. Principals must be models for both teachers and students minus the rigid, autocratic personality who views achievement as strict discipline and high test scores. I want a principal with a strong mind that is curious, playful, imaginative, creative and kind. A strong principal will actively involve parents and other community members who can help improve our students' chances for successful lives. An effective principal will not accept things as they are now, but will continually work toward what could be.

The most imaginative individuals in our society are not encouraged to teach and even fewer imaginative people go on to become principals of our schools. Those of us who work with imaginative administrators are very fortunate because we are more than likely working toward a common instructional goal. In my case, it is working toward making our self-selected whole language program viable.

For many years I had been experimenting with my curriculum and how best to get children to think without stifling their joyous sense of wonder and without losing my sense of humor or effectiveness. Our new program addressed many of these concerns, but there was research and a whole body of knowledge that I had only limited access to. Being involved in the day-to-day operations of my classroom left me little time to research current teaching trends and new methodologies. When my daily schedule changed and included teacher training in the form of modeled lessons, including informative handouts and relevant professional books, I got exactly what I had been hoping for. The modeled lessons offered new ways of doing my job more effectively, with more fun. Teaching became easier and my students enjoyed learning more. I found the time and energy to take related courses I had not found possible before. I finally had the support system I needed to play a full role in the whole language program.

In this case, the principal's sense of self-worth and integrity were not threatened by co-workers who possessed broad expertise in the area of curriculum development. Moreover, he showed a willingness to allow the most qualified personnel to take over an enormous and very exciting job of program implementation. His decision embodies the creative intelligence required of effective principals allowing us to work toward our shared goal.

Anita Hayward
MA, Education, MA, Educational Administration, Project Assistant/ Resource Teacher, Downer Whole Language School, Coordinator of Professional Development School Program, 1990–91. (Downer Whole Language School was designated Center for Excellence for Students at Risk, *by the National Council of Teachers of English, 1991.)*

Andrew E. Dubin

Adi Lapin
Writing Specialty Teacher, Downer Whole Language School, Coordinator of Professional Development School Program, 1990–91

The prevailing mythology holds that a principalship must be all things to all people, thus fulfilling a tremendous array of roles and functions. In addition, as the movement to restructure our schools gains momentum, this same principal must be able to gather and apply all the information and professional skills necessary to precipitate and sustain change. Is this possible? Can one person realistically and successfully carry out such a task?

At our large, multi-ethnic, inner-city school, the principal met this multifaceted challenge through teaming, strategic delegation and the use of a complementary and consistent information transfer system. He validated, backed up and garnered community and district support for curriculum change in order to establish a climate where innovation became the modus operandi and where members of the staff could realize and work toward fulfilling their roles in the change process.

Most importantly, the principal was not the sole change agent; rather, he was the primary member of a change team. This reflects the findings of Hall and Hord in their study, *Configurations of School-Based Leadership Teams* (Hall and Hord, 1986). In examining the roles of principals in effecting schoolwide change, Hall and Hord described and defined a phenomenon they discovered, in action, while conducting their study. They found that in schools where meaningful and sustained change had occurred, a clearly defined, dynamic change facilitating team assumed the roles and fulfilled the functions necessary for schoolwide improvement. Just as the authors found and labeled the essential roles of the change facilitating team as First CF, Second CF and Third CF, so did they exist in our school improvement process. The principal, serving as First CF, managed the change team by sanctioning, monitoring, pushing and approving the curriculum and climate adaption, while simultaneously telling relevant others, i.e., the community, central administration, etc. Moreover, he constantly reinforced both professionally and emotionally, his staff's efforts toward change.

As the project assistant/resource teacher, responsible for state and federally funded programs at the school, the co-author (Hayward) had both the opportune role and technical curriculum expertise to assume the position of Second CF. In this role she worked with teachers to create the new program vision under the auspices of meeting the everyday and ever expanding challenges of inner-city teaching. In other words, they took the state and federal resources (Chapter 1, SIP and LEP) and used them to establish a coherent research-based, whole language program that would reflect and meet the needs of their students. As Hall and Hord so aptly observed, she had to push, coach, train, and most importantly, provide the resources necessary for teachers to have what they needed to fully implement the change. She redefined and consolidated the traditional program model from after school inservices for teachers and pull-out programs for students to an in-class, demonstration teaching program that combined staff development and services to students. Of course, she kept her central office supervisors informed and encouraged their involvement.

Two people shared the role of Third CF. The resource teacher mirrored her role as demonstration teacher/staff developer, thereby max-imizing their effectiveness. The vice principal sanctioned and reinforced their work by approving, encouraging and applauding each individual teacher's response and progress. In addition, because he had recently come from a more traditional, less dynamic school, he was able to help his teachers see and appreciate their own real classroom gains and person-al professional development.

Fortunately, several years into the process, when the resource teacher (Third CF) decided to return to graduate school, the co-author (Lapin), another project assistant/resource teacher, was able to join the team. However, she joined as a co-Second CF because of her similar role and function at another aspiring whole language school. As a result of this previous experience, she came aboard not only as a trainer, but also as a designer, pusher and provider of resources. Moreover, because her tech-nical expertise complemented and extended that of the original Second CF, she was able to invest the program with another essential com-ponent, namely, a standardized, process writing program.

The Principal, then as First CF and manager, spearheaded their change facilitating team. He identified the skills and expertise of each team member and organized the team accordingly. He provided for consistent interaction and planning among the team members and re-gularly interfaced with ultimately important external CFs (district person-nel). He met the essential challenge of delegation, that is, he delegated strategically and maintained the necessary connections with all his team members. Specifically, he trained the Second CF to administer and utilize the state and federal programs' time, money and opportunities for train-ing as a consolidated basis for change. Guiding all, was his emphasis on operating a smooth, positive and effective internal organization that facilitated change.

The team dynamic that he so effectively managed was based on the clear, effective gathering and application of all the research and practical information essential to the change process. It revolved around the inter-play of clearly defined, yet overlapping roles; the goal being clarity of the program vision and the regular, active and accurate exchange of informa-tion through the open planning and frequent interaction of the team and staff.

The principal functioned as the CEO of our organization, providing and utilizing the necessary ingredients of an effective change facilitation team. Like other successful organizations, ours was guided by a clear mission and an operational plan flexible enough to strategize, revise and refine our change movement as new information came into play. As our experience of becoming the first school board approved specialty school of the Richmond Unified School District indicated, change is essentially utilizing and extending skills and resources while putting new information into practice.

Reference

HALL, G. and HORD, S. (1986) *Configurations of School-Based Leadership Teams*, National Institute of Educaton R&D Report 3223.

Key Points

1 Proactive decision makers involve teachers in the decision-making process because they are aware of and respect their expertise.
2 A proactive principal is one who directs an effective organizational process.
3 A proactive decision makers is aware of information sources appropriate to the needs of the school.

Discussion Questions

1 How do these exemplary teachers view effective proactive principals?
2 When they speak of the principal as a 'change agent' what do they mean?
3 What leadership traits are identified by these teachers as important for proactive decision makers?
4 In what ways have they identified 'reactive' principals?
5 How does a proactive principal instill a desire for teachers to grow professionally?

Chapter 6

Conclusion

What conclusions can be drawn from the information provided by the authors of this anthology? Are there emerging traits that are reflective of proactive principals and effective decision makers? Do the programs identified in the text demonstrate quantifiable leadership traits so that training approaches for administrators can be enhanced? Are specific information sources utilized by effective, proactive leaders? What is the relationship between the education reform movement and proactive decision making? These questions, which served as the catalyst for much of the focus for the book, have in large part, been answered by these contributing authors. The following concluding remarks will capture some of their ideas and comments.

While most authors identified the need for technology to be utilized in amassing and analyzing information essential to proactive decision making, most practiced a hands-on, people generated information approach. In this way, they were able to both collect the requisite information and interpret, extrapolate and sift through it on a personal level, which they found missing from the hard, tangible data reflective of charts, tables and 'numbers crunching'. This is not to say that they felt that computer technology should not be utilized. To the contrary, they felt that it must be utilized to provide for a complete picture for proactive decision making. Certainly, as identified in all projective reports, the need to predict demographic changes, integrate programming and scheduling, reorganize financial allocations all require more expedient and exacting strategies that can only be effectively accomplished with the use of computer technology. And the greater the understanding of the available technology, the more able the proactive administrator will be in determining its use in the given situation. Although this awareness emerged in the various interviews and section offerings, the central information gathering device employed and articulated by these successful decision makers was the one-to-one contact, the personal, more intimate connection between them and those significant others.

What of the reform movement and in what ways do these proactive decision makers, these educational experts, feel it will evolve? Will it change the status quo? I believe there was considerable variance in their responses as to whether the education reform movement will result in: significant change in the type of education provided; the difference in the levels of skills attained by graduating students; the structural/systemic changes needed for long term improvements; and likely increases in funding for K-12 education. While very creative and highly effective programs were identified that addressed successful application regarding more effective redistribution of funds for programs, better preparation of underrepresented students for high school completion and college entrance, improved integration and involvement of community groups in school processes and decision-making, it was clearly stated by most authors that the macro-organizational structure still required enormous overhaul. Business interests were extremely anxious, angry and becoming increasingly assertive in their desires and efforts to assist schools in meaningful change. The need for accountability at all levels must be clearly delineated so that areas of weakness can be more readily identified and remediated. To this end, the need for collaborative committee work among school sites, districts, community constituents, business groups, governmental agencies and institutions of higher education must continue to be stressed in order to reflect the respective needs and appropriate strategies to reconcile school problems.

While the information on proactive decision making provided by these high powered decision makers and analysts was extremely useful and informative, it did not reflect a departure from other successful practices noted in the literature on effective decision making. Perhaps that emerging characteristic needs to be articulated again in this text. With a society becoming more competitive, technologically oriented and rationally based, the need to create a supportive environment, a system that allows for personal conduits of information flow, which fosters enfranchisement not alienation, is greater now than ever before. The system needs to socialize its leaders and those aspiring to leadership positions to understand that proactive decision making, that is, effective leadership, requires interpersonal planning processes. The role of principal as autocrat/CEO no longer reflects healthy or effective leadership. Organizations that are structured to centralize decisions and disconnect those making the decisions from those who are impacted by them, are dysfunctional. Organizations must be predisposed in philosophy and aligned structurally to allow for shared decision making and decentralization.

The system requires the principal to be *facilitator/CEO*. The system demands the incorporation of complex information sources, data bases, spreadsheets, programming, to support objective analyses of problems as identified by teams of experts — teachers, resource specialists, special education teachers, and department heads — but guided by the facilitator/

CEO. He must be architect of the vision and one of the key players, but only one, whose role must be elastic in order to meet the changing needs of a complex school system and society. As indicated earlier, schools have the companion expectation of changing society and, at the same time, reflecting it. It is clear that the principal as facilitator/CEO is the role demanded by our schooling system in order for it to function effectively.

In addition, the principal will likely be more of a *politician/CEO*. Because of the need to make more of the fundamental decisions with constituent input at the school site, he will likely need to politic more in order to have various groups of his community 'buy into' his decisions. Traditionally, decisions are often made at the district level and so he would be relieved of some of the responsibility associated with those specific decision-making sources, committees, teacher groups, business interests, etc. Now he must be particularly artful in managing and directing the host of needs that will be desired by these divergent groups. This will require expert political planning to effectively manage the organizational system and strong human relation abilities to sensitively work with people cooperatively and supportively.

The principal will need to be highly skilled as an *entrepreneur/CEO*. Specifically, he must be highly cognizant of additional funding sources, available grants, scholarships, endowments, categorical funding, and so on at the local, state and federal levels to support school programs and activities. Because he will have a stronger leadership role in deciding budgetary allocations and thus be aware of appropriate placement of such funds, he must also be competent to regenerate these funds outside of the initial funding sources. Schools are experiencing inconsistent funding opportunities from all sources and so the entrepreneur/principal must posture himself to anticipate these limitations and be proactive in his planning. Financial creativity, linkages with business communities and broadening information sources in these contexts are areas to develop for the entrepreneur/principal.

The principal will likely be coordinating and integrating far more social services, which will be inherited by and housed at the school, in order to address the myriad of student-related social problems. This will entail serving as the school consultant for the needed support services for children who have emotional and/or physical disabilities, legal problems they must reconcile, health related concerns and financial needs. The presence of legal, financial and social agencies at the school site will likely increase and demand that the principal play a *consultant/CEO* role. This will likely be the most unique role since the social services offered at the school site wil be site-specific. This is clearly an emerging role that the principal will play.

What do these roles suggest for the principal? Are they very different from the traditional role identified in the literature? In many fundamental ways, the role of the principal will be different, particularly in the area of instruction. The most recent research regarding the role of the principal suggests that he play the role of instructional leader. It suggests that he should be directly involved with instruction, constantly monitoring teaching effectiveness, curriculum design and other areas focused on program content. Of course, this is an important role and one in which he will be involved. I believe, though, much of this responsibility will be delegated to teacher experts at the school site. He will be a part of the evaluation process since he will be accountable for all school activities, but it will be more of an indirect leadership role in this area. Reliance upon support expertise in personnel and utilization of appropriate information sources (the computer/technology application for additional input) will be the working structure. This calls to mind the significance of his support team, those personnel who will share the responsibility for making these curricular and pedagogical decisions. This will truly give 'teeth' to the shared decision-making initiative being espoused at all levels. It also gives added attention to the notion of accountability. This is a vital area that must undergo careful review. If a principal provides an atmosphere where there are professional growth opportunities and meaningful involvement in the school processes for teachers, on all levels, the definition of principal accountability and evaluation must be re-assessed. Clearly, when the principal assumes a new role and teachers do as well, new ways of analyzing, monitoring and evaluating those roles will be required.

The role of the principal in the wave of educational reform provides the most exciting opportunity for those aspiring to leadership positions. He can provide the vision to move a school and community in an innovative and progressive way. In a time when the pace of the world activities and technology is only transcended by the complexities that underscore them, a principal can shape, alter and direct lives around him. It is a profession haunted by prohibitive conditions, but propelled by the idea that it can produce change. What other profession offers such promise?

Index

DATE DUE

JY28'9			
SE 99			